Broken Mast

I0101981

Broken Mast

Changing Course for the Capitalist Ship

Evan M. Baumel

GLASSBLOCK PUBLISHING

Copyright © 2014 by Evan M. Baumel

Foreword copyright © 2014 by Colleen Callahan

All rights reserved. No part of this book may be reproduced in any written, electronic, recording, or photocopying without written permission of the publisher or author. The exception would be in the case of brief quotations embodied in the critical articles and reviews and pages where permission is specifically granted by Glassblock Publishing or the author, Evan M. Baumel.

Glassblock Publishing
Wellington, Florida

www.evanbaumel.com

Although every precaution has been taken to verify the accuracy of the information contained herein, the author and publisher assume no responsibility for any errors or omissions. No liability is assumed for damages that may result from the use of information contained within.

The contents of this book are copyright of their respective owners. All images were legally obtained and edited by the author. The writings and opinions of this book are solely that of Evan Baumel, and do not reflect those of Glassblock Publishing or its affiliates.

Cover design adapted from: *United States*, James E. Butterworth (1817–1894)
Photography credits:

Page 4, Eric M. Baumel; Page 17, Victorgrigas, Wiki Commons; Page 29, Lisa Brewster, flickr.com; Page 37, Evan M. Baumel; Page 51, kanu101, flickr.com; Page 60, Alberto G. (albertogp123), flickr.com; Page 72, Shutterstock.com; Page 88, Stefan Fussan, Wiki Commons; Page 100, 401(K) 2013, flickr.com; Page 111, Tim Wilson, flickr.com; Page 121, Evan M. Baumel.

Baumel, Evan M.
Broken Mast: Changing Course for the Capitalist Ship/Evan M. Baumel;
Foreword by Colleen Callahan
Includes bibliographical references

ISBN 978-0-996-01600-1 (pbk.)
Library of Congress Control Number: 2014936550
1. Economics 2. Public Policy 3. Current affairs

To my mother Lori, my father Eric, my sister Rachel, and my brother Sam...

...to the town of Wellington, Florida...

...and to the American University community.

For fostering (and tolerating) my passion for policy

Contents

Foreword

By Colleen Callahan

"Economics is a study of mankind in the ordinary business of life," as Alfred Marshall, the famous nineteenth century British economist, described it. This book represents an effort to carry this simple idea into the twenty-first century, a period which seems to face only complex social and political problems. Despite the challenging landscape of current public policy issues, economic principles can add insight to the debates even though economics cannot always provide clear solutions that all will embrace. The level of popular discourse will be elevated as it incorporates the economic way of thinking.

The goal of Evan Baumel's book, which was completed to partially satisfy the requirements of the American University Honors Program, is to connect recent scholarly economic research with controversial topics currently facing the United States. It is an ambitious project, written to be understandable to the general reader and to provide links to more specialized literature.

The scope of this ambition is demonstrated by the panoramic view of the issues confronting the American economy. First, extensive consideration is given to the basic question of how an economy is organized, with the author making a coherent argument setting forth the strengths of the capitalist system. Second, the numerous flaws characterizing capitalism in twenty-first century America are identified and seen not just as defects but as serious threats to the future of the system. Proposing remedies for these threats is the prime reason for the subsequent chapters.

Arguably, the most serious dangers are the long-run challenges, such as income inequality, climate change, and health care, which cannot be solved over the typical political cycle that may last only a few years. Economics may be able to provide a roadmap which can be used to help the general public formulate reasonable approaches to addressing the threats to the current system.

At its core, *Broken Mast* illustrates the long-ago sentiment of Alfred Marshall. Economics is used as a guide to the decisions faced by people in the ordinary business of life. This book makes a significant contribution to the level of public discourse and provides a way forward for the long-term viability of the American economy.

Colleen Callahan is an Associate Professor in the Department of Economics at American University's College of Arts and Sciences.

Acknowledgements

First and foremost, I would like to thank Professor Colleen Callahan for her assistance throughout the development of this book. Her insight provided me the ability to focus on key topics. By reviewing the economic concepts presented, she ensured that the words in this book resemble the general consensus of economic thought.

I would also like to thank the faculty and staff of the American University (AU) Honors Program. The Honors Capstone project gave me the opportunity to present this as an example of my academic work.

Many thanks to Nathan Williamson for crafting my experience at American University. Nate tailored my curriculum so that I could spend my last year in undergraduate academia pursuing topics and projects that interested me. In addition, I would like to commend the staff and faculty at AU's School of Public Affairs, for enhancing my understanding of the political world.

A deep appreciation to the following professors for providing their expertise in their relevant fields: Kiho Kim, Karen Knee, Amanda Fuchs Miller, Matt Glassman, Jaiqi Liang, Arthur Shapiro, Roger Streitmatter, Chris Edelson, and Shari Maclachlin. I also want to recognize the AU College Democrats, as well as AU Eco-Sense, for exposing me to a variety of important political, economic, and environmental issues.

I would like to offer a sincere thank you to the communications team at Greenpeace and Public Citizen, for providing the opportunity for me to explore the intriguing realm of political communication. In addition, I want to acknowledge the office of Congressman Ted Deutch for helping me recognize my strength as a writer.

With love, I thank my mother and father: Lori Hope Baumel and Eric Baumel, MD. Aside from being wonderful parents, they were the catalyst that inspired me to begin work on this project. They also provided assistance on the more technical aspects of publishing. I am forever grateful to my brother Sam and my sister Rachel, for providing moral support during this project.

Back in Florida, I want to salute the following teachers, mentors, and other figures I looked up to growing up in Wellington: Paula Sigmond, George Sink, Karen Clawson, Scott Zucker, Paul Gaba, Robert Rainaldi, Richard Fletcher, Karen Deacon, Kristi Gibbons, Sharon Willcox, Barbara Lieberman, Beth Smalling, Lynn Pernezny, Maureen Werner, Lynn and Russell Nagata, Dominick Brandine, Terri Gilstad, and Kathy West.

Notably, I want to express my gratitude to Florida State Senator Joseph Abruzzo and Palm Beach County District Attorney Dave Aronberg, for providing the experience necessary to validate my passion for politics. They continue to serve as role models for those interested in public service, as they defend the interests of the citizens of South Florida.

A special thank you to Krista Martinelli, editor of *Around Wellington* magazine, for providing my first journalistic experience in publishing. In addition, my sincerest appreciation goes to Murray and Dolores Rosen, Daniel Kraft, Harry Bayron, James H.M. Woodward, and Rabbi Stephen Pinsky for their guidance.

Finally, I thank all of my family and friends, who have supported me throughout this project.

Introduction

Smith's Legacy

IN 1776, THE SAME YEAR the American founding fathers signed the Declaration of Independence, a Scottish philosopher named Adam Smith published *The Wealth of Nations*. The book discussed the source of a nation's prosperity, and laid out the fundamental ideas that modern economics is based on. Economic concepts that high school or freshman college students are taught all originated from a single book. It serves as an all-encompassing source of economic foundations, which define the basic structure of a free-market, partially regulated Western economy. His theories surrounding the industrial developments that were taking place all over Europe signified a shift from a mercantilist national agenda to a capitalistic one.

The legacy of Smith's work is ever-present. To this day, capitalism has emerged as the best-known system of trade, triumphing over the totalitarian socialist methods of the Soviets and other forms of exchange. It was not divine will or national superiority that allowed the United States to remain standing at the end of the Cold War, but the fact that capitalism allows for room to innovate and change depending on the circumstances.

The capitalist system we use today is far from perfect. The markets cannot exist without a functioning regulatory system, strong sense of personal and financial security, competition, and the drive for innovation and technological breakthroughs. In addition, there is no purpose to growing the economy if the majority of individuals do not see the benefits of their hard labor. Unrest and dismay are growing around the world, and there are few signs of improvement.

We are at a crucial point in human history. The United States faces a great dilemma that cannot be solved without the cooperation of businesses, consumers, governments, and all other economic players. These problems range from local issues such as private debt to the earth shifting impacts of climate change. All of these challenges are related to or affected by current market practices, and can only be solved by applying an economic perspective.

This title of this book, *Broken Mast*, refers to the main source of movement and momentum of pre-industrial ships. Currently, our capitalist mast is beginning to show signs of weakening. The problem is that we need to fix it mid-trip, or else we will remain stranded and lost as an economy. While this book cannot offer panaceas for our woes, it can highlight some of the greater challenges we confront and how to approach them.

My prime motivation for writing this piece of non-fiction stems from my desire to propose solutions to the economic and political problems the world faces. The sweeping changes that we are about to discuss will require a significant personal and financial investment on the part of the global society. The best means to achieve this goal is to write about these issues and help people understand how it affects them.

Before Our Journey

There are a few notes about this book that I would like to point out. First and foremost, this work is directed toward readers who are at least familiar with the basic elements of economics and government, and have a passing understanding of policymaking. I will try to limit any technical jargon and explain more complicated concepts.

Chronologically, I will first describe what defines modern "capitalism," and how it compares to other systems. This book will then cover some of the systematic issues that our economy faces, such as recessions, political instability, and chronic unemployment. We will then focus on education and health care, two major sectors responsible for economic growth that also suffer from internal and external dysfunction. Finally, we will discuss more long-term subjects that impact the markets, such as monetary policy, debt, income inequality, and the environment.

Although the book is structured to flow as a single continuous writing, it is essentially a series of essays on a variety of subjects. Each chapter is broken down into sections, allowing for natural pauses and demonstrates a clear transition from one topic to the next. It is important to note that these economic threats are interconnected, and taking steps to solve one problem will undoubtedly affect another.

Since this book is written from an American point of view, the language of this book will reflect that fact. However, there will be several instances where I will refer to people or institutions outside of the United

States. For instance, in the chapter regarding environmental degradation, a global problem, all nations will need to take simultaneous action.

Finally, as we pull our anchors and begin our journey, remember that these thoughts and essays represent my viewpoint on these issues. These problems require individuals with many perspectives to come together and discuss potential solutions. Only through a public conversation on these issues can we overcome obstacles that may prove hazardous to our voyage into the economic sea.

Chapter 1

A Brief Explanation of American Capitalism

Times Square New York, NY, July 22, 2008

TRADE, SINCE THE BEGINNING of human society has been the cornerstone of the development of civilizations. Before professional message services and the Internet, the marketplace was the best place to discover new cultures, products, ideas, theories, and inventions. It was also the source of many conflicts, as barter quickly proved to be an ineffective method of valuing goods.

For thousands of years, trade and commerce has guided the fate of every civilization. Trade between European and Asian countries prompted exploratory expeditions to find the best routes for exotic goods. Even before Eric the Red and Christopher Columbus discovered the realm separated by the Atlantic and Pacific, Native American cultures had established trade routes and centers where different tribes would exchange goods and wares. Large African civilizations built their empires on the wealth earned through trade with other tribes and peoples.

Today, the world economy has greatly grown in size and interconnectivity. At the time of this publication, the world GDP in 2012 stands firm at around 72.44 trillion dollars, a huge leap from only decades prior.[1] Human factors, such as health care, education, and personal well-being continue to improve as time passes. Technological innovation continues to push the boundary of our market potential. From a macroeconomic perspective, the "invisible hand," Adam Smith's concept that as markets grow the general welfare rises as well, has clearly shown its presence.

However, there are far too many problems in the world to accept these changes at face value. Economic inequality within and among nations has grown to its greatest extent in modern human history. Conflicts and wars continue to arise over both trivial and essential matters. Potential environmental changes, many of which were caused by our drive for growth, pose a threat to humanity itself. The standing of our economic and political institutions, many of which have lasted for centuries or even millennia, are showing signs of decay.

In this chapter, I will describe the structure of the modern capitalist system, and reveal the inherent benefits and flaws that arise from it. The United States and other developed countries generally follow the same formula of having the markets determine the flow of goods and services. Before discussing why rehabilitation of our capitalist system is necessary, we must first explore why we follow a market-based economy in the first place.

Capitalism, in its purest form, is a remarkably effective system of evaluating products and services, and offering just compensation for the labor invested. However, as with all social theories, there is one prime reason why achieving a pure capitalist state is impossible or discouraged: the reality of human desires, behavior and rationale. We are not only incapable of trusting each other to keep our desires and possessions in check, but also deceive ourselves in believing that we can accurately predict what the future holds. That is why civilizations have, over time, instituted regulations on market behavior, and created third parties (i.e. governments) to resolve disputes.

Demand the Supply, Supply the Demand

If you have ever taken an economics class, you will know that the basis for determining the quantity of goods and services sold is the Law of Supply and Demand. The point where supply and demand intersects is considered the equilibrium point, and should reflect the market at the present time. Under ideal conditions, the equilibrium is at a point where the price of a commodity is low enough for consumers to willingly buy it while simultaneously high enough for the company (or companies) involved to make a net profit.

Supply and demand regulates the price of goods in such a way that *usually* prevents any large-scale surpluses or shortages. If the price rises beyond what consumers think is rational, they will stop purchasing it, which eventually forces prices back down. If prices are too low, vendors will raise their prices until either they reach profit maximization or they are able to meet the demand sufficiently. While there are other intricacies behind movements in prices, supply and demand still remains the backbone of the marketplace.

The key word for the past paragraph is "usually." There have been many instances where external factors lead to a wide fluctuation in supply or demand, causing markets to respond in a negative direction. For instance, at the time of writing this chapter there is a severe shortage of Ritalin, a medicine used by people suffering from Attention Deficit Disorder (ADD).[2] Supply is currently low due to excessive demand, and the medical field suffers from price inflexibility, meaning that it is incredibly difficult to reduce demand through price changes.

Another example of markets working in unforeseen circumstances is the demand for oil. A decrease in supply results in an increase in price, and for most commodities the demand gradually falls. However, since oil is a vital part of our economy, and cannot be easily replaced with a substitute, demand went up instead of down. As a result, the price of oil and related goods (i.e. gasoline, plastics) skyrocketed. The oil supply shock was one of the primary causes of hyperinflation during the 1970s, and raised prices of many goods during the early 2000s.

In principle, supply and demand does a wonderful job of balancing our desire for goods with the market's capacity to satisfy that desire. However, there are cases where the behaviors of businesses and/or consumers do not respond according to economic expectations. Remember that economics is a social science, despite having a scientific approach and philosophy. Economists and market analysts often make assumptions that rely upon unpredictable behavior. This is how market bubbles and recessions occur.

This Land is My Land

Private property is often associated with homes and buildings, yet in economics and law it is defined as anything possessed by an individual or group. In other words, everything you have purchased is truly yours, and cannot be taken away without an equitable transaction or legal penalty. Not only does this societal rule discourage stealing, but it also encourages individuals to stockpile or hold assets for future use.

One of the fundamental requirements for a stable market is the protection of private property. While this may seem to be an arbitrary requirement, giving private individuals and businesses the irrefutable right to own what they purchase is a tenet for economic growth. Without this guarantee from the government or the companies who sold the products, consumers would be hesitant to make such transactions in the first place. Guaranteeing ownership of property, such as land or goods, builds the framework necessary for investment and innovation. Individuals and companies are more willing to take risks on something they own.

Of course, this does not mean that owners have absolute free reign to do what they desire with their purchased goods. Over time, all capitalist countries have placed limits on the scope of viable activities, and prohibited actions that could impact other people's property. For instance, significant environmental destruction is not a permissible action, even if it only initially alters the area within a company's boundary. This is to protect surrounding owners from factors that are not controlled within a set perimeter, such as air and water pollution.

Protecting property rights not only encourages productivity, but also discourages actions that may hinder a competitive market. For instance, copyrights and patents ensure that those who create new ideas and products are the sole proprietors of those goods. If such rules were not in place, any company could copy or steal an idea and earn revenue that is intended for the original creator.

Innovation can flourish in a system that safeguards proprietary ownership of ideas or products, but taking this protection too far can also hinder it. If the law only allows a single corporation to produce a widely used product, it stifles the opportunity for competitors to improve that good or service. Patents and copyrights have expiration dates to allow new companies to innovate established commodities, without fear of violating the law.

The definition of protected property is a constant struggle for governments and markets. Many of our most important products came to be only because they were protected, while others were introduced or greatly improved upon once these safeguards expired. When deciding the boundaries of ownership, it is essential for policymakers to provide the best atmosphere for innovation and the public well being.

Competent Competition

One of the fundamental tenets of capitalism is the concept of competition. A healthy market for most goods and services has multiple businesses directly selling a particular product. Economists hope that these players will be pressured to regularly improve their products and lower their costs to gain more customers. In addition, giving consumers the choice of where they buy their products forces businesses to monitor or imitate the successful tactics of their competitors.

Competition relies on several factors to be sustainable, such as the concept of information symmetry. This term describes giving consumers information about a product and the company that sells it. Equipped with this knowledge, customers can make a rational choice regarding which vendor they will purchase from. In addition, if one company decides to significantly raise or lower prices, consumers and other businesses are able to appropriately respond due to easy access to prices across the market.

In addition, the number of competitors (and the size of their market share) must be high enough to prevent one business from easily taking over the sector. The exact limits necessary for healthy competition depend largely on the companies involved or the industry itself. It is also possible to have too many competitors, which could force prices so low that companies would be unable to earn enough revenue to pay for wages and other expenses.[3]

If there were only one or a few companies in charge of selling a specific product, the benefits that we see from a competitive market would disappear. These monopolies have total control over their good or service, and can charge whatever price they choose is appropriate. Since there are no alternative options, a monopolistic company can choose which businesses or customers are able to purchase its products. This can easily lead to inefficiencies due to irrational favoritism and corruption, and demotes the incentives for innovation.

While monopolies of non-essential products are of no major concern for regulators, there have been many instances where monopolies over economically important products have arisen. The post-US Civil War period is notorious for having certain businesses maintaining firm control over sectors such as transportation, finance, oil, steel, and tobacco. While these monopolies led to many great developments in infrastructure and economic growth, they were also politically unstoppable. [4]

In modern times, the federal government has the legal power to "bust" or dismantle monopolies and divide companies into several smaller competitors. While this action may seem greatly disruptive and damaging to the economy, the market has historically quickly responded to these changes for the better. For instance, some suggest that the division of AT&T in 1982 paved the way for an ultra-competitive telecommunications industry.[5] It is unlikely that the market for cell phones or internet-based companies would have exponentially grown if they were forced to deal with such a monopoly.

With few exceptions, every business in the United States is involved with direct competition. However, as the market becomes more globalized, companies must not only deal with local pressures, but from international forces as well. The regulations foreign companies face may be greatly different, which makes it difficult for smaller competitors to enter into the market. One of the questions that must be answered in the 21st century is how to maintain competition across a complex legal landscape. We will explore this conundrum in a later chapter.

Live Free, Buy Free

As an economic institution, capitalism is not only one of the most efficient systems, but also offers the greatest freedom to its participants to sustain and improve themselves. The income earned by individuals or companies can be used in any capacity imaginable. In addition, having a greater choice in the goods one can purchase encourages a competitive marketplace.

One could assume that those against a free-market system (and they do exist) argue that having too much autonomy with disposable income could lead to irresponsible behavior. Indeed, there are many examples where people have seen an increase in income, only to see it disappear due to reckless purchases and a lack of fiscal concern. However, it is important to note that the freedom to purchase allows new ideas and products to flourish, which generates greater economic activity. For instance, Elon Musk, the former co-founder of PayPal, has used his vast fortunes to develop companies in a variety of new industries.

History has shown that stable democratic governments and capitalism tend to work well together. Both rely on the concept that an individual's worth is based on his or her capacity to effectively use the resources given to them. In addition, democratic institutions tend to exhibit the least amount of corruption, a prime source of stagnation and unsound economic policies.

In a democratic society, where an individual's rights are protected, people psychologically feel more comfortable taking actions that may deviate from what is considered the norm. In economics, this translates into a ripe entrepreneurial spirit, which encourages people to take financial risks. Indeed, many of the largest economies today thrive because they have environments favorable for new businesses.

On the other hand, weak personal freedoms or unstable governments make it difficult for the majority of its citizens to advance themselves. Some countries have established democratic institutions, but are plagued with political favoritism and corruption. These governments make it difficult for the average individual to take financial risks, as the barriers of entry for starting a business are greater for individuals outside the politically powerful elite. Totalitarian regimes that benefit from a vast pool of resources and land are capable of high GDP growth, but mismanagement and oppression usually cause this expansion to be a short-term trend. It is rare to find a non-democratic state that gives most of the wealth accumulated to the lower and middle class, rather than creating a class of concentrated wealth.

The Labor Hot Tub

Market incentives encourage all parties involved to provide the maximum output for their labor. While we may have an innate drive to take part in productive work, the potential for personal gain provides the extra motivation necessary for ambitious individuals to take significant risks. For economists, the incentive to expand the yield of one's labor is the cornerstone of efficient trade, which allows the economy to prosper.

Free-markets also respond relatively easily to the demand for new labor. Individuals advance their skill set in the hopes that having a diverse range of talents and expertise will make them attractive candidates for high-paying positions. In the event that there is a shortage of workers in a certain sector, the best way to entice new workers is to incentivize that labor force with more income and benefits.

Unfortunately, as markets change and technology leads to greater and more efficient products and services, there will inevitably be instances where a particular job or sector falls out of favor. In economics, the phenomenon of jobs being eliminated due to the evaporation of old markets is known as "creative destruction." While many workers are capable of learning skills related to their field, there are those whose isolated specialty leave them vastly unprepared to find new positions.

The good news is that the modern economy enables driven individuals to acquire the necessary skills for new work. Many educational and training resources can be found for free online, or can easily be accessed in most regions across the United States. In addition, there are government programs that allow people to receive stipends for undergoing job training. Some businesses encourage workers to take time off to learn new skills, with the promise that training will boost the productivity of their employees.

The globalized marketplace has provided many bountiful opportunities for companies to tap the world's workforce and sell their products to foreign consumers. Unfortunately, it has also allowed companies to hire workers in countries with lax labor and wage laws, where workers are paid lower salaries than employees in developed countries. While the workers in these factories are paid wages far higher than the average laborer in that country, it promotes the exploitation of foreign labor for the purpose of greater profit margins. Providing ample opportunities for laborers around the world while ensuring these workers have basic rights will be one of the primary challenges of the 21st century.

Innovation Exploration

Capitalism has many forms, but they are all based on the principle that the marketplace is the best means of maintaining and improving civilization. Advancements in medicine, technology, and education foster the potential to greatly improve the productivity of labor in a variety of fields. For businesses, this leads to reduced costs and higher earnings, and for workers this could translate into higher incomes.

Developments in technology have accelerated greatly over the past few decades. Consumer computer technology has gone from being a pipe dream in the mid-20th century to accounting for 4.8% of total US GDP in 2012.[6] Innovations in renewable energy continue to greatly reduce the cost for these alternative fuels, which is necessary to combat widespread environmental harm from other sources of power. The advent of 3D printing is showing promise as a means to develop parts necessary for consumer goods, significantly lowering the costs of manufacturing.

There are many channels where innovation and technological advancements can occur in the modern marketplace. Some companies have a research division to create products that blow competitors out of the water in terms of quality. This, in turn, forces those companies to create similar or better products at the same or lower price, which benefits consumers the most.

The drive for technological innovation has both beneficial and harmful consequences, as we see in the realm of employment and technology. While innovation significantly lowers the costs of manufacturing, most of the costs saved are a result of laying-off workers whose jobs were replaced or streamlined. In addition, the deterioration of online privacy allows companies to peer into the private lives of current and potential employees. This not only enables businesses to regulate the personal activities of individuals, but it also harms current job applicants who currently display risky or immature behaviors online.

The fast pace of growth in sectors such as telecommunications and computing make it increasingly difficult for new players to enter these markets without a significant resource investment. This leads to only a select few corporations holding control of almost all of a particular market. Over time, an industry with reduced competition and fixed players becomes stagnant, and discourages further investments in potentially innovative or beneficial technologies.

Technological innovation will most likely lead to the most important economic developments of this generation. Capitalism is one of the strongest forces behind this trend, so it is important to preserve the incentives for companies to invest in new products. However, we must also account for the costs of such innovation through maintaining the open environment of the current tech culture and carefully enacting regulations that control the worst effects of these changes.

Parental Regulation

Capitalism, for all of its benefits, does have a tendency to create harmful by-products as time passes. Businesses may intentionally underpay their workers to maintain ultra-low prices, pollute the local environment, create low-quality goods, or make fraudulent claims about their products. While the market is capable of correcting some of these forces on its own, it often takes a strong outside player to enact necessary changes. To ensure that the principles of a fair and competitive market are enforced, there must be a neutral third party to resolve disputes and implement rules and regulations.

Thus, the institution of government remains a vital player in ensuring the stability of the economy. While there are many important discussions regarding the scope and scale of regulatory powers in the modern economy, few intellectuals and economists would argue for a complete division of governments and the marketplace. It is necessary for this body to help resolve civil suits between individuals and companies, as well as maintaining security, both physically and psychologically.

The prime benefit of (limited) government involvement in the market is the lack of a strong profit motive. While governments collect taxes and engage in limited commercial activity, the salaries of public workers are not usually tied to the amount of money collected or earned. Their prime motive stems from a desire to utilize their expertise and labor for public good, while providing a means to support their family. When it comes to solving conflicts between companies, prohibiting commercial fraud, and enacting regulations, the most neutral party is one that has little to no financial ties to the impacted industries.

That is not to say that a government does not seek to maximize the productivity of domestic output. Tax income is usually derived from commercial activity, and economic downturns directly reduce revenues the government can receive. Without adequate funding, some necessary public sector spending, such as security and regulations, would be cut, which could have an adverse effect on the economy. As a result, it is natural for governments to intervene to stimulate the market during recessions, or discourage inflation through reduced government spending and contractionary monetary policy.

To ensure fairness and responsible activity in the marketplace, it is necessary that the cost of violating regulations is harsh enough to discourage damaging behavior. The government has the power to enact financial penalties on companies or individuals involved in rule breaking, which sends strong signals to investors and consumers to avoid transactions with them. In addition, more serious financial crimes such as fraud or scams can lead to imprisonment. Governments, however, cannot be too selective when it comes to enforcing its regulations, or else it may unjustly give leverage to certain corporations over others.

Thus far, I have spoken as if economic regulations are a necessary and proper use of government power. While I agree with this assessment overall, I would be foolish to assume that there may be circumstances where overregulation may lead to adverse outcomes. Redundant inspections and unnecessary protocols can be a significant resource drain for these companies, and once government bureaucracy is in place it is nearly impossible to remove.[7]

The best check to determine the appropriate amount of regulation, taxation, and enforcement is through elected leadership. If consumers or industries feel that there are faults with the current government, they can easily replace (or threaten to replace) officials responsible for the error. Elected governments also guarantee regular changes in personnel, preventing elected public servants from exploiting their position for personal gain.

A growing challenge businesses face involves foreign governments and laws. As multi-national businesses expand in new countries, they must verify the stability and trustworthiness of the current regime. In places where bribery and corruption are rampant, it may be difficult for long-term growth to take hold, as most of the wealth gained often ends up in the hands of high-level officials. The United States government may have many systemic problems, but remains one of the best institutions in the world to regulate and secure international business.

Capital Headaches

Thus far, we have covered a wide variety of benefits and advantages a market-based economy offers for society. However, capitalist systems are not immune to adverse human behaviors, and at times encourage destructive actions. If left unchecked, the free market offers endless bounties, but may lead to widespread human suffering to achieve such success.

No one is innocent when it comes to abusive corporate behaviors. Many economists point out that consumers "vote with their dollar," meaning that they reward businesses for providing cheaper or more efficient products. For most companies this translates into creating better products and improving efficiency. Unfortunately, there are some businesses that interpret high profit margins as a sign of lackluster concern for human atrocities, such as underpaid workers or unsafe conditions.

Capitalist countries universally experience periods of economic expansion and decline. The so-called "business cycle" refers to a relatively consistent period of rapid growth followed by a recession. Oftentimes, these downturns are triggered by inaccurate speculation by investors rather than a physical cataclysmic event that impacts supply or demand. We often forget that the economy is a human construct, and is subject to the psychological state and opinions of its participants.

Many economic calamities occur due to greed blinding individuals and their businesses. The drive for ever-increasing profit margins creates an atmosphere of delivering short-term gains by any means necessary. Prior to almost every recession, there is a sense of endless growth and revenue. This encourages highly risky behaviors and sacrifices caution for the sake of maintaining momentum.[8] To this day, we have yet to come up with a systemic plan to counteract an economic crash, as it is nearly impossible to predict the cause or date of a collapse.

One of the most visible faults in the free market is the growing income inequality, a trend that is evident in almost every capitalistic country.[9] In classical economic theory, income disparity is a byproduct of a difference in productive capability, and different incomes reflect the effort put in by each individual. In other words, there are those that conclude that the only reason that poor people exist is due to a lack of effort on their part. This may have been true when the United States was largely an agrarian economy, when everyone needed to provide some amount of manual labor to survive. However, this concept of laziness on the part of lower-income individuals is inaccurate and imprudent, and distracts us from the threat wealth disparity poses to the economy.

The source of such twisted logic is the belief that success is entirely dependent on the drive and productivity of an individual worker. It is true that a motivated individual is more likely to pursue higher paid work. However, many of the wealthiest individuals on the planet have achieved extraordinary success through pure luck. These entrepreneurs obtained their wealth by connecting with rich individuals, who assisted in propelling their businesses. Warren Buffett, founder of Berkshire Hathaway and a man who knows success firsthand, describes this phenomenon as the "ovarian lottery," where the family or socioeconomic class you are born in determines your likelihood of accomplishment.[10]

People are a poor judge when it comes to assessing risk and reward, regardless of their education or business experience.[11] As a result, our economic indicators may not reflect the full picture. There are factors that cannot be easily converted into cost or value. Thus, taking a wrong action may lead to greater financial or societal loss than initially predicted.

The clearest example of our capitalist system ignoring a direct threat is the degradation of the environment. It is extremely difficult for economists, businesses, and policymakers to identify the economic value of preserving our natural resources. Part of the problem is that we do not recognize how vital an ecosystem or species is until it is gone entirely. The good news is that after centuries of ignoring environmental damage, economists are just beginning to recognize the long-term threat that ecological damage poses to the economy.

The capitalist ship is a sturdy vessel that is capable of traveling far distances. Thus, it is important to inspect and repair any damage it incurs along the way, or we face the risk of sinking the economy. We may never be able to solve all of the problems that arise from the modern free market. Only through careful analysis and some degree of human understanding can we can avoid contributing to societal ailments. If our capitalist system fails to accommodate the world's needs, there will be nothing else to maintain the order and progress we have accomplished.

...Or is there?

Chapter 2

What Else is There?

The hammer and sickle, a well-known symbol of Socialism, on a fence in Moscow, Russia, June 9, 2012

IT IS ABUNDANTLY CLEAR THAT CAPITALISM is an efficient, but deeply flawed system that needs constant checks and balances for it to work for everyone. Placing heavy emphasis on economic prosperity can do both great and terrible things to a country, especially one as individualistic as ours. Given the current state of affairs, it is not surprising that many people are wondering if the American form of capitalism is the best system.

However, if capitalism has so many faults, is there a different or similar school of economic thought that could work better? The answer is less certain than we would prefer. Markets are derived from human interaction and trade, and are reliant upon the character of the players themselves. While some economic systems have advantages over others, none really stand out as remarkably efficient and fair.

Still, it is important to examine these other systems and identify their strengths and faults. This chapter focuses on alternatives to American capitalism, and discusses the reasons why we have not and will not adopt these economic alternatives. You may realize, as the chapter progresses, that our system incorporates many ideas and practices from other theories. This is primarily because our markets have evolved over time to challenge these other schools of thought, and have adopted some of the best aspects of non-capitalist ideologies.

Merry Mercantilism

Before what we know as modern capitalism emerged, many countries followed an economic system known as mercantilism. The very name implies that "merchants" would play a heavy role. However, the basis behind mercantilist systems is a powerful national government agenda. The countries involved (mainly European) took part in a heavy global "trade war," where the goal was resource and military superiority.

For mercantilist countries, the goal is to have more valuable materials and goods (i.e. gold, silver, spices, etc.) than their neighbors. This is maintained through a strong standing army/navy, exclusive trade routes, and other policies aimed to promote national businesses. Private competition was present in mercantilist countries, but most large-scale trade was accomplished through state-based companies.

Mercantilism is considered the forerunner to modern capitalism primarily due to its core philosophy. It sees trade as the prime method of maximizing productivity, which lead to significant revenues for the state. However, the drive for productivity gains assumed that increasing wealth for the treasury of a country would, over time, trickle down to better security and services. Unfortunately, most of the money obtained through "empire-building" ended up in the hands of aristocracy, which fueled domestic unrest.

A mercantile country also created an arbitrary class system where colonies were technically and socially inferior to the mother country. This almost guaranteed that the work performed by the colonists and lower-class citizens contributed to wealth accumulation at the top. In addition, trade under mercantilism led to widespread corruption, racism, and the dissolution of legal rights, which only exacerbated the problems this system caused.

One sign of the decline of mercantilism was the American Revolution. When news spread of the successful separation of the American colonies from Great Britain, European leaders worried that this event would trigger unrest in other colonies worldwide. Over time, the companies that lead the mercantile march would dissolve or form other private companies.

Today there are no countries that consider themselves mercantilist, and former empires transitioned to modern capitalism or other economic systems. While there is still a national drive for economic superiority, most countries are more willing to rely on trade with other nations. The rise of global markets and the decline of monarchies across the globe eliminate the desire to return to such a system.

Mercantilism lasted only because the countries practicing it were able to exploit what seemed to be unlimited resources. In addition, communication technologies during this era were still rather primitive, and so it was difficult for the impacted colonies to resist until the imperial forces had full control. In modern times, the world's resources are increasingly limited, and following the practices of mercantilism today would spawn international distain.

Centrally Planned Economies

We know that one of capitalism's prime weaknesses is the unequal distribution of income. Though there is nothing wrong with this inherently, there is a plethora of examples of hard-working individuals being paid minuscule wages. This leads to certain groups or occupations that are guaranteed to suffer in poverty, while others are paid on an exponential level. For countries that seek an end to this problem, they may choose to take measures toward implementing a centrally planned economy.

Countries that follow this principle provide basic services in return for part or all of a workers wage. For instance, in many European countries, health care is a service provided or subsidized by the government, paid for through higher taxes. The key theory propelling the development of state-based markets is the fact that the government does not have the profit motive of a private company. Thus, it will avoid cost-cutting measures or unreasonable prices that end up hurting the consumer. Additionally, unlike private monopolies, a government-run sector is directly or indirectly accountable to the people who use the service, though this only works if the country is democratic in structure and practice.

Supporters of centrally planned markets stress that the benefits that arise from giving the government domain over certain sectors can help the economy in the long run. For instance, although after-tax wages may be lower, consumers would not have to worry about earning enough to provide for themselves or their family. This lower burden could potentially lead to greater efficiency, or allow certain industries to grow from the greater percentage of discretionary spending. Advocates would note that technological progress has allowed certain necessary resources to be plentiful enough to facilitate equal distribution.

Of course, centrally planned economies also suffer from a fundamental flaw: it must still follow the rules of supply and demand. If the government guarantees a certain service or product, then they must predict almost every change to its demand or supply. The Soviet Union, the fundamental example of a predominantly centrally planned system, regularly faced shortages due to bureaucratic inefficiencies on the supply side.

In addition, the high taxes faced in centrally based economies need to be broad to ensure the full payment of governmental services. This leaves a smaller portion of income left for discretionary purposes. Most investments for new products come from firms or individuals who have a significant portion of their capital free to spend. As a result, the drive for technological innovation slows, as less money is spent on new products. There is also the threat of taxes growing so high that wealthy households decide it is no longer worth their effort to increase their income. This would significantly reduce tax revenue, which leads to fewer services, and creates economic stagnation overall.

Another challenge to the central planning model is that economies that employ it are not resistant to external market forces. The most recent recession is the clearest example of this challenge, as many countries saw a considerable decline in income and employment, leaving less money to properly cover its expenses. Some governments that cover health care are faced with extreme inflation in the health sector, meaning that it becomes harder to deliver this service without cutbacks or higher taxes.

The United States has mostly avoided centralizing markets, but there are certain sectors where the US government (federal, state, or local) has complete control over a certain sector. For instance, transportation routes are significantly controlled by various governmental agencies and laws, and are paid for through taxes and traffic fines. Radio wave frequencies, a valuable commodity for electronic makers and media companies, are strictly regulated by the US government.* In addition, private corporations provide electricity, but the prices they charge are completely determined by state officials. The United States may not be a centrally planned economy, but it still incorporates a great deal of control over a significant portion of certain markets. Whether this leads to a positive outcome for American citizens is up for debate.

Marx and His Children

Karl Marx was truly a product of his time. He was raised as the industrial revolution was in full steam (pun unintended), and was deeply troubled by the terrible conditions many laborers faced. Marx was horrified that the owners of factories and businesses were making incredible amounts of money and gaining too much power, while simultaneously making the lives of their workers increasingly strenuous. Based on his personal philosophy and observations, he theorized that the capitalist system was one of class struggle, where the wealthy exploit the poor for personal gain.[1]

Marx was no simple writer or theorist. He had a firm understanding of history, economics, politics, and philosophy, and developed his principles based on the social circumstances of the time. He held the view that, in the near future, workers would grow so frustrated and desperate that they would overthrow the "owners." This broad label not only included the wealthy aristocracy, but also the government, which was seen as perpetuating the interests of the rich. In place of a demolished capitalist state, he suggested the community establish control through cooperation.

The theories Marx and his colleague, Fredrick Engels, laid out in the *Communist Manifesto* spawned a variety of political worldviews that still shape the thoughts of economic theorists. Many political revolutions are led by leaders waving the socialist banner, and there are still countries whose governments emerged from a socialist agenda. Unfortunately, there has yet to be a truly sustainable socialist system, and successful socialist revolutions have usually dissolved states into totalitarian regimes.

Though most economists and western philosophers dismiss many of their assumptions, Marx and Engels's description of worker dissent accurately described the threat of ignoring the plight of lower-class workers. Anti-communist paranoia tends to rise most prominently during times of extreme prosperity, as the increased concentration of wealth was a prime motive for communists to start creating chaos for the system. During the US Progressive Era, some advocates for better working conditions concluded that passing labor laws and busting monopolies was the best means of fighting the socialist threat.[2]

Technically there are many branches of Marxist thought, but for this chapter we will focus on three main schools: Marxism (also known as Socialism), Leninism, and Market Socialism. During the early stages of the Cold War, it was difficult for intellectuals to study or examine the mechanisms of communism without being considered an enemy of the state. However, now that the Soviet Union has dissolved, there is no risk in admitting some of the advantages that these theories hold, along with their glaring flaws.

Socialism (Est. 1848)

One of the fundamental tenets of Marxism, which causes the most distress to capitalist governments, is the method by which socialism is achieved. Almost all leftist groups that subscribe to Marx prefer revolutionary methods, such as violent overthrow or civil disobedience. Once the revolution is successful, the citizens will establish a new socialist system, where the people control the means of production and reap its benefits. Value and currency are discarded, as the workers will gain only what the community gains through their labor.

Socialism, along with similar far-left ideologies, emphasizes the equal treatment of all workers who provide something for society. The class structure established by capitalism will crumble when the working masses rebel, and everyone's importance will depend on their productivity. Under a Marxist system, the concept of personal value is abolished, as the laborers own the means and gains of production.

Such equality allows for goods and services necessary for the community to be distributed evenly. Because it is difficult to truly measure the "value" of labor, socialism abolishes the old system of compensation. Instead, every worker who contributes to the community's well-being is entitled to basic commodities for his or her family. The benefit of this system (assuming it functions as intended) is that it reduces the widespread poverty seen in many capitalist economies.

The greatest flaw of socialism, and one that applies to many similar ideologies is that it places a high amount of faith in its players. While most individuals seek what is best for society, it is not safe to assume that people will simply follow the doctrines of communal idealism. Successful socialist revolutions opened the doors for political and social infighting, as seen after the fall of the Russian Czar in 1917. In addition, when capitalism fails, the means to organize labor in a productive capacity becomes difficult without strong leadership.

Many economists argue that no personal profit motive would lead to worker apathy and decreased productivity. Marx retorted that what is best for the community is also best for the individual.[3] Lack of participation results in worse conditions for the state as a whole, and so laborers will be motivated to act for their own well-being. This could be possible, but it also creates a scenario where a worker must follow the doctrines of the community, which hinders the development of new ideas or suppresses dissent.

While it is safe to assume that we naturally prefer to live in groups and form societies, there is no guarantee that once a socialist community is established no more conflicts will occur. Marx assumes that human conflicts arise due to economic disparities, and that crimes that take place under capitalism will disappear under a communist system. However, the motivations for crime stem beyond money, such as political, social and cultural differences, and will most certainly remain if a socialist revolution removes the established system of laws.

There is also the problem of technological innovation. In a capitalist society there are several motivations for improving the technology we have: more efficient products, greater profit margins, opening new markets, and other incentives. Marx believed that socialism would occur at a time when we have reached our innovative apex, when industrial progress can go no further. However, the changes that Marx observed in his era were only the beginning of a massive scientific and technological renaissance. The only way for socialism to emerge today under Marx's intentions is if we no longer have the resources to innovate.

Leninism Schism

When the Russian Revolution was in full steam, Vladimir Lenin was amongst the men leading the charge for a new socialist state. Lenin, a political writer, anti-Tsarist revolutionary, and adamant Marxist, wanted Russia to become a beacon for communism. However, when he finally took over as leader of the new Union of Soviet Socialist Republics (USSR), the revolutionaries suffered an incredible dilemma: how to peacefully transition to socialism.

However, Marx never specified how exactly a socialist society was formed, and so Lenin attempted to fill in the gaps. According to Lenin, for socialism to emerge, there needs to be a socialist state to formulate the specific structure of the new communal union. This state would only be temporary, and must adhere to the socialist principles of equality and societal well-being. Once a system is established, the state is dissolved, and the people will live under a new communist ideal.

Even if Lenin was willing to adhere to his plan for a socialist society, it never came to fruition. Lenin died only seven years after the revolution, after which Joseph Stalin took over the Russian government. Stalin took the Soviet Union in a dramatically different direction, leaning towards a strong centralized economy based on mass production and militarization. This is a trend many other socialist states followed soon after, with bloody and irreparable results.

Leninism suffers from some of the same problems that socialism faces, in that it places far too much trust in the intentions of political leaders. Unlike democratic capitalist states, there are no checks on the power of government, and it is easy for strong personalities to assume total control of the socialist state. To date, there has been no example of a socialist government transitioning into what Marx or Lenin envisioned. The most successful "socialist" state, China, has long since abandoned its goal of a socialist transition in favor of a one-party semi-capitalist system.

Market Socialism: Far-Left Middle Ground

At first, the term "market socialism" would seem to be an oxymoron. Socialism itself was designed by Marx and Engels to be the inevitable implosion of the capitalist regime. To have a free market would inevitably lead to the same inequality and suffering that a socialist revolution intended to avoid in the first place.

However, market socialism still follows Marxist principles of equality and communal well-being, and serves as a natural reaction to the dilemmas described earlier. Theoretically, market socialism breaks down the concept of personal ownership of goods and class structure, and simultaneously preserves free market principles such as supply and demand and the law of value. In other words, the primary differences between market socialism and capitalism is the method in which profits are distributed.

Instead of several corporations organized through hierarchical structures, with executives being of a higher class, every aspect of one single company is owned and directed by the public. This corporate entity will seek to maximize its profits and innovate like a traditional business, with multiple companies serving different functions in society. However, when the profits are fully accounted for, the money is directly funneled to the general public, which can be used to maintain or improve public well-being.

In addition, market socialism can allow for trade with outside countries and economies. Since one key flaw of socialism is its isolationist view, this system protects itself by keeping up with the innovations of the outside world. However, all wealth generated through international trade can only be used to improve the community and productive capacity. In keeping with Marxist ideology, the participants of this system assume that society only benefits from the hard work of everyone involved. Thus, high compensation is unnecessary as an incentive for upward mobility.

The problem this ideology faces is that it is difficult to create on a larger scale. In modern times, there are many economic sectors vital to our standard of living, and no single entity can account for every market. In addition, competition is the cornerstone of ensuring efficiency, as it forces companies, communities, and nations to constantly improve themselves. Having a single company represent the community inspires romantic images, but destroys incentives for further growth.

Another attack against market socialism revolves around the possibility that workers would have a reduced incentive to place their full effort into their roles, as personal well-being does not dramatically improve with personal production. Theoretically, while hard work may improve the lives of everyone in market socialism in the long term, its immediate effects are not present to the average worker. This causes them to lose focus and become disinterested in their job

Last Laugh for the Leftist

By now, it is apparent that Marx and Engels's vision of a sustainable communal state where everyone is treated equally is impossible to achieve when capitalist ideals are demoted. Human selfishness and greed make it impossible for socialist states to last without a strong central power to enforce laws, which often leads to totalitarian regimes. Thus, every historic attempt to create a large-scale socialist state either reverted back to a capitalist system or collapsed outright.

However, Marx's writings are a stern warning against an unchecked capitalist system. The markets provided (and still provide) many productive benefits, but also led to widespread human suffering. Wealthy individuals during the industrial revolution were isolated from the worst abuses of their businesses, and had no incentive to encourage income growth amongst middle and lower-class households. Both the US and Western European countries experienced rapid urbanization, which created unsafe conditions for many cities.

In some ways, the development of labor rights and regulations were a natural response by governments to prevent the predictions Marx envisioned. Because of strict health, safety, and competition rules, many industrialized markets experienced improvements in productivity and technological innovation. In addition, the rise of automation and machine labor eliminated many jobs that were often the source of dissent.

It is impossible for socialism to properly form in the modern global economy. However, we are seeing rising discontent from consumers and citizens around the world, all of whom seek to get rid of corrupt political and business leaders. It is in the best interest of all governments to consider the demands of its citizens, or else risk a violent overthrow that yields no benefit for the economy in the short-term.

Legally-Enforced Lawlessnes

When many people think of anarchy, they associate it with chaos, lawlessness, and destruction. Yet advocates of an anarchist economy claim that anarchy is, by definition, the simple absence of government. This system is appealing for those who find the political and commercial realm as a selfish system that favors a certain class of individuals. Anarchy is similar to Marxism, but it follows a different set of values. Instead of focusing on the abolition of class and inequality, it focuses on the demolition of the current authority, the leading source of corruption. Concepts like private property and value are thrown away in a communist society, whereas anarchy goes one step further and dissolves authority entirely.[4]

Anarchy relies on resources to be expansive enough for individuals or groups to establish and expand their own territory, which they defend from exploitation by outside forces. It is certainly possible for peace to exist between two anarchist groups, as long as both parties accept the boundaries of their territory.[5] There is some merit to arguing that some of the early American colonies are examples of attempted anarchist societies.

However, the moment conflict arises within or between anarchist groups is when chaos tends to emerge. The only way to resolve conflicts is either through a "ceasefire" on either side, or the total annihilation of the opposition. Thomas Hobbes declared this society of unending fights for land, resources, and power to be a period where life was "solitary, poor, nasty, brutish, and short."[6] The inevitability of quarrels justifies the existence of a "third party" to resolve conflicts.

An anarchist system that serves to benefit all involved in today's world would be difficult to achieve. Almost everyone has come to terms with a government's role in resolving internal conflicts and defending the nation from crime and foreign threats. Even citizens living under oppressive, corrupt governments seek to replace the current system with something resembling well-run capitalist states.

Many self-proclaimed anarchists today draw their political views from their opposition to the current political and business elites.[7] They seek to end what they see is an unjustified infringement of their natural rights and freedoms, and endorse the overthrow or overhaul of major institutions. Because the wealthy and politically powerful have ignored the demands of the people, they argue, the only viable option is to take their discontent to the streets.

However, it is rare to find anyone who follows the dogma of anarchy to its logical extreme. Few anarchists bring to the table alternatives that could maintain order and security. This instability and uncertainty is one of many reasons why anarchy is difficult for the average person to find attractive, and leaves only radicals to take the helm of far-left movements.

Individuals who consider themselves anarchists typically tie this ideology with other systems. Anarcho-socialists are people who want seek to demolish the government and set up a community based on mutual aid. Anarcho-capitalists, on the other hand, seek the dissolution of government to allow the free market to operate normally. It is rare to find intellectuals who follow the doctrine of a pure stateless society.

Markets Make the Most Sense

We can see from the examples above that capitalism has lasted because other economic systems have either failed or have shown poor results in comparison. Thus, we can conclude that the United States, at least in the short term, should remain a regulated capitalist economy. Perhaps one day we will discover a new economic school that can cover some of the systemic issues that capitalism leads to. However, these theories are the domain of economists and policy experts, and are unlikely to arise until we have a better understanding of the behavioral tendencies of consumers.

We should focus less on altering the structure of our capitalist ship and instead seek to change its trajectory. Capitalism has proven to be resilient, and there is no incentive to change vessels in the middle of our voyage. However, even if our captains of industry stay the course, there will still be troubled waters ahead.

*Believe it or not, there is a "limit" to the spectrum of radio waves capable of broadcast and reception. As a result, the Federal Communications Commission (along with the International Telecommunications Union) is in charge of choosing which sector or company has access to the spectrum.

Chapter 3

Recessions, Depressions, and Market Failure

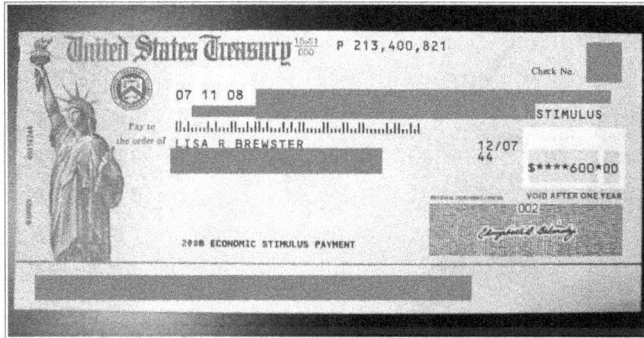

2008 Economic Stimulus Act stimulus check, July 16, 2008

WHEN THE FIRST SIGNS OF FINANCIAL COLLAPSE were apparent in early 2008, President Bush and Congressional leaders decided to take a preventative measure to boost consumer confidence and avoid a market downturn. The Economic Stimulus Act authorized the US Treasury to send tax rebates to every middle and lower-income American household. Although the individual checks were small compared to per capita income, policymakers believed that they were sufficient enough to encourage spending in the marketplace.

One study by economists Christian Broda and Jonathan Parker proved that the checks sent to households did temporarily boost consumer spending.[1] It is possible to assume that these results proved that this measure reduced fears that a wide-scale economic collapse was imminent. However, another study shows that most people who received the checks saved it or paid off prior debts, which is the opposite response to what policymakers originally intended.[2]

If lackluster consumer confidence was the main factor responsible for economic slowdown, the stimulus would have been an adequate fiscal response. Economic growth would have steadily returned to normal levels, Congress would have claimed victory at preventing a market failure, and the potential for mass layoffs would have been greatly diminished. However, hindsight has revealed that the problems undermining the economy were far more complex than anyone could have comprehended. The interplay between the financial sector, the housing market, government regulators, and other major corporate players was so lucrative at the time that most people ignored the storm clouds ahead.

This chapter focuses on the phenomena of market failure. We will examine how the most recent recession (known by some as the "Great Recession") originated, as well as the repercussions of policies enacted before and after the crash. It is nearly impossible to predict future economic downturns, as they originate from a variety of market forces. However, there are many lessons from the most recent crash yet to consider, and these could potentially reduce the pain endured during the next downturn.

Economists have generally agreed that booms and busts are a natural part of the market. Recessions are often a sign of overly optimistic speculation and market imperfection, and give major economic players the opportunity to correct their mistakes. However, this most recent downturn revealed clear faults in the way our economy is structured. Unfortunately, many of these cracks have yet to be sealed, and could stall economic growth or trigger another downturn in the near future.

Unforeseen Dominoes

There are many political and economic factors spanning over two decades that ultimately contributed to this recession. It is impossible to delegate blame to a single source. Financial firms had an incredibly lax credit policy, and created complex financial tools to profit from the growth of housing prices. In addition, government policies originating from both political parties encouraged the development of the housing bubble. Consumers overestimated their ability to pay back the loans they received, and engaged in risky activities to take advantage of the rapid growth of property values.

There is no particular moment when everything fell apart, but the first omen was when the price of houses stopped rising in 2006-2007.[3] This growth halted as over-speculation in the construction industry resulted in an oversupply of houses. Simultaneously, faulty credit ratings for subprime mortgages led to lower-than-expected returns, which severely undermined the value of this market. These factors, along with others, contributed to a dramatic drop in property value. Ultimately, households nervous about the prospect of paying off upside-down mortgages responded by reducing their spending overall. One by one, financial titans who had made lucrative profits off of the housing bubble and easy credit fell flat.

What followed was one of the worst economic downturns since the Great Depression. Countless companies merged, declared bankruptcy or cut payrolls, leaving millions of people without jobs. Banks refused to lend to some of their most reliable clients, leading to an unprecedented credit freeze. Without access to loans, many small and medium businesses were unable to stay open, forcing them to close shop. In metaphorical terms, the economy had the equivalent of a heart attack, and needed immediate aid before permanent damage took hold.

By September 2008, it was clear that Congress had no choice but to save the economy from dire circumstances. Political leaders on both sides were involved in crafting the rescue package, which was necessary to encourage firms to loan once again. Even the two presidential candidates, Senators Barack Obama and John McCain, were brought in to ensure the initiative's political support in Congress. The Emergency Economic Stabilization Act, known colloquially as the "bank bailout," was enacted as an emergency bill in October 2008.[4]

Most people assumed that the bailout was simply a $700 billion dollar government handout for the banks to do as they please. However, the design and implementation of the Troubled Asset Relief Program (TARP) was far more complex. TARP funds were not simple checks or loans, but served as insurance for lenders who were terrified of loaning money to businesses and consumers at a loss.

Overall, the TARP program did successfully restart the credit market, and ultimately encouraged banks to begin loaning again. However, such rapid recovery did not trickle down to other sectors, as banks moved slowly to assist smaller businesses. In addition, the firms that survived the crash resumed using the same risky financial tools that contributed to the recession in the first place.[5]

Post-Downturn Stress Disorder

The process of restoring the credit market was rather sluggish. Most banks that used funds from the bailout ultimately started loaning again, but only to major corporations and other "safe" firms. Many smaller, local banks were either closed or purchased by larger national chains. It was not until 2010 and beyond until the financial sector showed strong signs of activity.

Meanwhile, the depressed housing market caused stagnation in the construction industry, as properties remained far below their peak value before the crash. In addition, many homeowners thinking of relocating elsewhere were stuck with higher mortgage payments for a house worth less than what they initially took out a loan for. These obligations are a significant barrier to normal consumer spending, and we still have yet to clear this hurdle.

Foreclosure rates slowed down soon after the crash, but there was little relief for the millions of homeowners who already lost their homes. Those who could not afford to pay their mortgages suffered from a significant dent in their credit score. Not only does a lower credit rating make it harder to take out another loan, but it also restricts these households from accessing resources that could improve their income, such as education. There was some relief from the government, but it was nowhere near the amount of damage incurred by these households.

Consumer spending remained tepid until it was clear that companies were willing to hire again. To boost economic activity, Congress and President Obama passed an $831 billion stimulus bill, which provided funds for a wide assortment of endeavors.[6] Though it included appropriations for construction and maintenance projects, it also provided tax breaks for households and businesses. The stimulus aided in improving consumer spending, but was not significant enough to address some of the chronic after-effects of this recession.[7]

Millions of jobs were either eliminated or had wages and benefits shrink substantially. While this is normal during economic downturns, the challenges the unemployed face today are far greater. Most of the jobs lost will never return, as they consisted mainly of low-skilled, medium-wage labor. In addition, companies have consolidated responsibilities into fewer positions, with employees taking on more work without an equal rise in income. Most workers have accepted these conditions, understanding that their prospects for a new job are dim in an ultra-competitive labor market.

The Fool's Gold Parachute

While the cause of downturns can vary, the government's reaction is usually the same. Congress implements short-term spending provisions and offers tax breaks, which eases the pain felt by consumers. After the government softens the blow to the bottom, the economy bounces back and everything returns to relatively normal levels. If there were any illegal or questionable activities that directly led to the calamity, lawmakers could introduce legislation that prevents similar actions from reoccurring.

However, the recent recession has revealed that policymakers and economists are unprepared when it comes to the aftermath of major financial crashes. The Great Recession was severe enough to completely undermine vital aspects of the market, and contributed to many of the problems seen in this book. Without a general plan to address these developments, we will continue to see slow, painstaking recoveries like the one we are experiencing as of this printing.

When looking at the standard measures of the market, it appears that the economy has returned to nominal levels of growth and productivity. However, reality paints a harsher picture, as unemployment remains stubbornly high and middle class incomes continue to stagnate. Such conditions would normally worry speculators and analysts, but the domestic marketplace has instead thrived in these conditions.

The problem with current expansionary policies is that it has mostly aided economic players at the top. Tax cuts and stimulus measures over the past decade have mainly benefited upper class households, and have provided only minor relief for middle class households.[8] While large companies and wealthy individuals have the potential to drive greater innovations and create jobs, they have not done enough to reverse the damage done during the recession.

In addition, the opportunities for small businesses to grow are minimal, as venture capital is insufficient in many regions of this country.[9] Hiring workers and obtaining inventory is an expensive ordeal, and financial firms are looking for businesses that can offer guaranteed and timely returns. This places significant barriers for new companies seeking to enter the market, and reduces the potential for new jobs. There are alternative means of funding for small projects, such as Kickstarter and Indiegogo, but no business can adequately rely on these methods without a loan from a bank.[10]

The rise of globalization has complicated the effects of traditional stimulus measures. Many of the jobs lost will most likely never return to the United States, as companies increasingly rely on cheaper labor abroad for low-skilled work.[11] The laws and regulations protecting workers overseas are weak compared to those covering American workers, and it is difficult to penalize companies who send jobs outside the US.

BS in Political Math

The government has the capacity and the authority to accelerate economic recovery, as it did during the start of the recession. Federal unemployment benefits and insurance provide a temporary shield for households facing hard times, allowing them to focus on obtaining work. In addition, many local and state governments offer tax incentives for companies hiring workers, reducing the costs of added labor.

Unfortunately, unemployment policies have become outdated and overburdened, and cannot address the core causes of a massive rise in unemployment. Because many lower-skilled positions disappeared or moved overseas, millions of people are unqualified for the modern job market. The time and savings necessary to invest in higher education or technical skills is not covered under safety-net programs, and obtaining supplementary part-time work would disqualify them from these benefits.

There are many conservatives who deplore the dramatic rise in government spending that took place during the first years of the Obama Administration. However, such concerns are not based on rational arguments, as it would have been fiscally impossible and unfeasible to enact stimulus policies while simultaneously maintaining a balanced budget. There is justification for allowing the deficit to rise during strenuous times, as long as politicians are willing to cut back on such spending later on.

The Federal Reserve has used extraordinary monetary policy measures to promote economic recovery. While these actions have been highly controversial, the Fed quickly realized that its conventional methods of stimulating the economy, such as lowering interest rates and buying back bonds, had proven insufficient for such a severe recession. Congress apparently gave up on expansionary fiscal policy while the economy was sluggish, so the Federal Reserve had to be creative, using measures such as quantitative easing to increase incentives for lending and growth.

The degree to which illegal activities led to this recession is rather negligible. Most of the profits earned prior to the recession were lawful financial transactions, and there is little evidence that banks intentionally violated the rules governing finance. It was poor judgment and risk analysis, not malicious intent, which destabilized the marketplace.

The regulations implemented or proposed after the recession were introduced in hindsight of these errors. New regulations, such as the Dodd-Frank financial reform bill, attempted to prevent this scenario from re-emerging. However, it is unlikely that these new rules will deter market downturns that originate from other causes.

How to Save the Future

All predictions anticipate steady, but slow, economic growth over the next five years, and all of the problems described above are slowly sorting themselves out. While this financial situation could have been worse, we have yet to completely understand how to adequately prevent some of the after-effects of a recession. There are important actions that should be taken before and during the next recession that could avoid many of the hardships we have endured.

Smaller businesses are an essential backbone of economic growth and innovation, and employ a substantial portion of the population. Reducing barriers for these companies, such as hiring and training incentives or lower corporate taxes, would aid them in their quest to prosper. However, banks must play their part and once again grant loans to these entrepreneurs. These financial firms are investing in safe or long-established corporations, making it difficult for new businesses to succeed.

On the supply side of labor, the government should tie unemployment benefits for those affected by economic downturns to learning new trades. Since many new jobs will be in the technology and energy sectors, local and state governments should establish training programs that teach these individuals essential skills in these fields. In addition, the unemployment programs currently available need to accommodate for the dramatic rise in part-time jobs. Such work should not disqualify someone from receiving unemployment benefits, especially when there are almost no openings for full-time work.

In addition, the financial market should avoid the temptation to return to the strategy of profiting off of housing prices. This places far too much pressure on housing prices and encourages excessive lending for homeownership. In addition, the government should have the authority to require banks to renegotiate on certain loans to protect homeowners from suffering a major credit score drop. There should also be temporary protections for homeowners who face the threat of foreclosure due to external economic conditions.

Instead of continuing expansionary policies or attempting to tackle chronic unemployment, Congress has cut government spending and instituted other contractionary measures. While these measures are necessary to reduce our deficits, they also undermine government assistance for those who lost their jobs during the recession. If Congress insists on maintaining a balanced budget while protecting the middle class, then it should at least cease further cuts to safety net programs such as unemployment benefits. Such spending is hardly considered "wasteful" after one of the worst downturns in almost a century.

Although new rules will do little to prevent future economic recessions, it is essential for the federal government to be wary to protect consumers from undue harm. Rough economic times may encourage certain companies or sectors to take advantage of vulnerable households. As a result, the creation of the Consumer Financial Protection Bureau (CFPB) was a necessary step to provide adequate oversight and serve as an advocate on behalf of the general public. Already, the CFPB has held corporations responsible for a variety of abusive tactics, and should be fully equipped to handle future financial challenges.

After moving at a rapid pace, the capitalist ship hit a reef and needed to pull itself out. Our vessel has traveled at varying speeds, and it appears that its pace is gradually increasing. However, unless we address some of the conditions that led to our unfortunate accident, this ship will continue to face similar obstacles. We will often need to travel in harsh conditions, but acting in advance can prevent further suffering for the inhabitants of this vessel.

Chapter 4

Political Perspectives and Paralysis

Crowd awaiting the Supreme Court decision in *National Federation of Independent Businesses v. Sebelius,* June 28, 2012

LEADAMERICA WAS A YOUTH CONFERENCE for high school students who wanted to experience a simulation of a particular field of interest. In the summer of 2007, I joined several dozen fellow young adults in Washington, DC, to participate in its Congressional Studies program.* By working with students from different states and with varying ideologies, we learned how to tackle some of the issues Congress was debating.

When it was time to participate in a mock Congress session, our group (a Democratic House) passed both of the bills we had worked on for an entire week. However, we were appalled to find that the other group (a

Republican Senate) had rejected our bills and passed their own. We felt betrayed. These were people who we met during meals and lectures, shared similar agendas, and worked together to find a compromise before our proposals faced the floor. In retaliation, we rejected their proposals, and partook in a stalemate that prevented any noteworthy accomplishments.

When the session was over, the program directors pointed out the similarities between our scenario and our political system. What starts as a petty dispute leads to a complex political battleground, with each side plotting to undermine the other. Considering how quickly the situation broke down in our simulation, and how the current political game has been played for well over a hundred years, it is amazing to consider how the government functions in the first place.

This chapter has two prime purposes. First, we will examine the current differences between liberal (also known as progressive) and conservative economic perspectives. It is important to acknowledge ideological differences, as it allows us to work with our peers who hold views that diverge from our own. Second, we will discuss the deep political divide between the Democratic and Republican Parties. Compromise is rarely an option unless the fate of economic stability is at stake, and our leaders seek every opportunity to dismantle and discredit their opponents.

Why are we discussing political dysfunction in a book that focuses on the challenges to our economic well-being? Political gridlock is becoming a growing threat to economic stability, and is increasingly affecting national and global markets. If the current trend of expensive and bitter political battles continues, it could compromise investments that are directly tied to the function of the United States government.

There have always been divisions in the size and scope of government spending and regulations. The Constitution, which grants and limits the power of the federal government, is intentionally vague to provide the greatest flexibility to adjust to new circumstances.[1] Though the words of this text has not changed, the interpretation of it has significantly evolved over time.

I would not be truthful if I stated that I did not display any sort of bias. I consider myself an economic moderate, but I often align myself with left-leaning coalitions on social issues like abortion, gay marriage, and immigration. However, I recognize that both the liberal and conservative camps have their fair share of fanaticism. I will attempt to represent the views of intellectual conservatism and progressivism in a fair overview. Regardless of your political affiliation, I encourage you to read the concerns and agenda of each side, and accept the limits of both schools of thought.

You Have the Right to Remain Wrong

The modern two-party system arose from disputes between Federalists, such as John Adams and Alexander Hamilton, and Anti-Federalists, such as George Mason and Patrick Henry. These two factions argued over a wide variety of issues, most of which pertained to the size and role of the federal government.[2] While the Democratic Party technically originates from the Anti-Federalist faction, the views of a "Democrat" have changed dramatically over the past two centuries. The Republican Party arose from the ashes of the former Federalists and Whigs, but has experienced a gradual ideological shift to the right since the post-Civil War era.

Today, the Democratic Party is generally a liberal-leaning movement, whose strength is derived from individuals who favor strong government actions and programs. While most Democrats believe in the benefits of the free market, they believe that the government should play an active role in promoting equitable growth and protecting citizens from corporate abuse.[3] Meanwhile, the Republican Party is composed of citizens concerned with a bloated federal government, and seeks to either reduce regulations and spending or return power to the states. There are many examples where inefficiency and unnecessary regulations waste taxpayer dollars, and the Grand Old Party (GOP) pledges to let the private market sort out most of our problems.[4]

In many ways, the two political parties cancel each other's ideological weaknesses. Conservatives tirelessly oppose efforts by some of the more dogmatic liberals to expand the role of government to the point of damaging economic growth. Progressives are keen to raise red flags regarding corporate abuse and unwarranted inequality, whereas conservatives often turn a blind eye. Exposing the worst aspects of each ideology allows voters to hold their politicians accountable for issues that concern them.

There is nothing inherently dangerous with disagreements regarding policy agendas. Many of the founding fathers disagreed on a wide variety of issues such as slavery and the scope of the federal government. They understood that it was essential for a democratic society such as ours to allow for dissent and differing opinions.[5] Without varying viewpoints, our nation would quickly become homogenous, stagnant, and unable to address new problems.

However, policymakers are defeating the purpose of ideological discourse by refusing to challenge each other's positions.[6] When you observe committee meetings or debates on the floor of Congress, almost everything stated is planned in advance. The very concept of "debate" no longer occurs within public forums, and everything is negotiated behind closed doors. In today's mass media frenzy, politicians cannot openly debate without being dissected by the pundits.

To combat this paralysis, politically engaged individuals should not only decide where they stand on these issues, but also understand the viewpoints of those on the other side. We will examine what each side stands for in terms of economic policy, and determine the danger of following either side to the extreme. While social issues are an important motivator for political loyalty, we will exclusively focus on the economic divide between liberals and conservatives.

Progress, Stage Left

The running theme of liberal economic policy is the role the public sector plays to protect consumers and workers. While economic growth will occur largely within the private sector, the government can still ensure that every citizen's quality of life improves in times of prosperity. As a result, progressives believe that the federal government has the responsibility, and thus the right, to intervene in ways not explicitly mentioned in the Constitution.

Liberals are generally in favor of strong regulations for businesses. The government is the only third party capable of preventing or punishing corporate abuse, and should have ample authority to control market activities. This applies to maintaining decent wages, mandating safety rules for hard labor, limiting environmental degradation, and providing benefits for disadvantaged workers. Without these protections, companies would have free reign (or even legal immunity) to engage in immoral actions for the sake of reducing costs and increasing profits.

In some ways, this position serves as a reaction to the conservative push to weaken or eliminate government interference in corporate affairs. Many liberals consider attempts at reducing regulations as a sign of corporate favoritism, serving only wealthy executives in their quest to exploit labor and resources. Though there may be some legitimate purpose to remove unnecessary regulations, progressives approach any attempts at deregulation with caution.

Whenever economic calamities arise, liberals are often the first to recommend government stimulus as a means of improving the economy. Progressives follow the doctrine that the markets recover too slowly when a recession strikes, and it is the duty of the government to reduce the pain endured by the consumer. As a result, they are far more comfortable with allowing the deficit to grow temporarily, under the assumption that policymakers can raise tax revenues when the economy improves.

Liberals offer strong support for unions and other forms of employee representation. Organized labor serves as the first line of defense against workplace abuse, and empowers workers to become politically engaged for greater benefits. While there is a legitimate purpose for unions to exist, conservatives note that the link between progressive politicians and organized labor is somewhat too close for comfort.

Turning Blue

Far-left liberals dream of the day when the United States joins the rest of Europe and offers a broad range of government services. They advocate for proposals such as government-sponsored health care, substantial worker protections, highly funded public education, and nationwide mass transit systems. For these progressives, such a system would not only improve overall quality of life, but also provide a means for greater economic advancement.

However, economic and political reality prevents many of these goals from occurring overnight, and there are legitimate reasons to oppose proposals for these programs. One of the prime reasons that we have not transitioned towards these progressive goals is due to well-established customs, industries, and infrastructure. In order to convince the public that new government programs will benefit everyone, these groups need to first convince voters and workers to change their behavior. Liberals have been overly optimistic regarding the possibility of more nationwide services, and they have failed in their endeavors because of it.

When making comparisons to other countries, progressives tend to ignore the factors that lead to successful implementation in these regions. The United States is a massive country with a highly diverse population. Implementing effective national programs requires a tremendous amount of resources, time, and labor. The only way to ensure success for these endeavors is to raise revenue through significantly higher taxes paid by all citizens.

Progressives argue that while the costs may be sizable in the short term, future generations will enjoy vast benefits from improved public services. Properly implemented programs could have a stimulating effect on the economy when completed, but it will still require a significant sacrifice from its citizens. There is also no guarantee that these services will run smoothly, and it is much more difficult to reduce government bureaucracy than it is to create it.[7]

Liberals frequently propose raising taxes on wealthy individuals as a means of funding programs that help those in need. While such a proposal is popular, conservatives rightly fear for the consequences of such measures. It is essential to remember that higher taxes overall will lead to less disposable income for these individuals. While the money spent by the government would stimulate certain sectors, depressed private spending would drag down economic growth.

The public debt we owe today is substantial in its own right, and the proposals mentioned above would only contribute to the size of the federal deficit. Since the federal budget is currently in a state of contraction, it is impossible to justify a dramatic increase in spending without raising taxes proportionally, a task few politicians are willing to accept. In addition, concern regarding the public debt (though passive) is near an all-time high, especially as programs such as Medicare and Social Security are growing at an unsustainable rate.[8] The worst-case scenario is that overspending could damage the credit of the United States government, making it more difficult to receive loans to pay for these services.

What's Right is Right

Generally speaking, a conservative favors a smaller government, which spends and taxes as little as possible. They argue that maintaining a strong, private market is essential to solving many of our social ailments. Competition between businesses is the greatest source of technological innovation and growth. Thus, the government should interfere as little as possible to allow Adam Smith's "invisible hand" to improve public well-being.

Conservatives do not want to eliminate government outright, and they understand that the prime purpose of the state is to provide security. They seek to ensure that government officials remain as separated as possible from the free market. Contrary to what some liberals may claim, the calls for reduced regulations and taxes mainly arise not from a desire to destroy government services outright, but from concerns against a bloated and inefficient public sector.

To conservatives, the public sector has grown at an unsustainable rate, and could potentially lead to greater economic inefficiencies in the long run. The federal bureaucracy is a massive organization, suffering from redundant positions, outdated infrastructure, and poor communication. Even if an agency works effectively, too much regulation could stifle profits and needlessly raise barriers of entry for new businesses, leading to diminished innovation and productivity.

In addition, government programs for the needy have created a long-term dilemma for the federal budget. Programs and protections for the poor and disenfranchised have rapidly grown in size because more individuals take advantage of easy-to-access benefits. As a result, our deficits have skyrocketed in the last few decades, a dangerous scenario for a society that will eventually have to pay for high debt.

Some conservative policy experts have concluded that the best method of reducing the size and scope of government is to advocate for lower taxes across the spectrum. Without higher revenues, policymakers would be forced to cut inefficient government programs, as well as reduce enforcement for unnecessary regulations. This may also encourage the government to adopt better practices and reduce overhead costs. Unfortunately, attempts to shrink the government through this method have been largely unsuccessful.[9]

Many conservatives are actually comfortable with welfare programs, but insist that any attempts of government assistance must be conditional to prevent abuse. They understand that giving unconditional aid to poor individuals, who often lack motivation, would best use these resources to find work.[10] Without strong incentives to seek employment, the government would be forced to care for entire generations of impoverished households, which provide nothing in return.

Depending on whom you ask, some conservatives prefer that economic policy decisions remain at the state level, rather than from Washington, DC. These "states rights" advocates argue that competition between the states would ensure the best environment for business growth and innovation. The federal government should only be involved in the private market if it is absolutely necessary to protect interstate commerce, as specified in the Constitution.

Limited Role Model

During normal or prosperous economic times, there is a strong case for implementing conservative policy. Because conservatism places extraordinary faith in the capitalist system, they rely on figures and messages that are clearly quantifiable. However, when it comes to non-economic factors, such as the environment, they either understate the significance of these subjects or reject them entirely. Such a move is dangerous, as it is impossible to account for non-economic factors until the damage has been done.

What we have experienced since 2007 has impacted society in ways that cannot easily be measured, and many conservative proposals today do not account for the dramatic changes that the economy experienced. For instance, limiting the government's intervention during the start of the crash would have been suicidal, as it would have left the financial market in shambles. While it was certainly possible for the market to correct itself without assistance, the damage would have severely wounded the global economy.[11] I will not debate the merits of greater financial regulation, but most arguments against it provide no real assurance that major players have learned from their mistakes.

The labor market has undergone a dramatic shake-up, destroying job prospects for millions of Americans. Many of those who rely on unemployment assistance or other programs do so because they have nowhere else to turn, and private assistance cannot fill in the gap. That is why it is perplexing to see the government cut these programs rather than expand them. Calling those in need "lazy" or "unmotivated" is an outdated messaging ploy, and does not reflect the demographics of those who have suffered from this recession.[12] The private sector shows no sign of relief for those impacted by creative destruction, and less aid is likely to greatly exacerbate wealth disparity.

The protection conservatives offer against overburdening government regulations and taxes is an important asset. However, the prime issue with this stance is that those who usually benefit from this safeguard are the wealthiest citizens.[13] The idea that wealth "trickles down" from the top is a strong conservative principle, but is also one that rarely translates into societal well-being.

The marriage between reasonable conservative economic policy and the proposals from conservative politicians is becoming increasingly distant. While respectable institutions call for reforms to currently existing programs, it is not rare to find politicians who seek to gut entire bureaus. Many individuals, from fiscal moderates to far-right activists, wave the conservative flag. As a result, inconsistent or contradictory policies often emerge within the same alliance. It is especially baffling to see Republicans attempt to reverse the Affordable Care Act, which mainly consists of proposed suggestions from conservative think tanks.[14]

Mutual Hatred

There are clear differences between liberal and conservative economic perspectives. While these two camps have similar goals for economic growth and societal stability, they disagree on the means to achieve it. Over the past few centuries, progressives and conservatives have passionately argued over the proper balance for public services and government involvement in the markets.

However, the fact that there are disagreements does not disqualify policymakers from having important discussions. By many measures, the 113th Congress has been one of the most inefficient sessions in our nation's history.[15] This is mainly due to the fact that the two parties, both of whom diverge on social and economic issues, control two separate chambers, and refuse to pass legislation drawn up by the other side. While there have been several points in history where two different parties controlled the House of

Representatives and Senate, few sessions have been as unproductive in terms of legislation passed as this one.

The argument could be made that our founding fathers did not want a government where policy is made at a rapid pace, and deliberately crafted a system that moves slowly. These safeguards, such as a bicameral legislature, frequent elections in the House, and the filibuster all exist to ensure that a minority voice would have the opportunity to fight popular but dangerous policy decisions.[16] Unfortunately, the lackluster performance of Congress has more to do with political bickering than the safeguarding of democracy.

The situation has deteriorated to the point where the United States government, long seen as a continuous body that would never fail in times of peace or war, has shut down three times within the past twenty years. Both parties continuously blame each other for failing their obligation to seek the best outcome for their constituents. Unfortunately, while trust in Congress has degraded, the same leaders responsible for this paralysis continue to be re-elected.[17]

The impact political gridlock has on the economy has been minimal thus far. However, the negative repercussions will only continue to increase as standoffs and stalemates become a regular occurrence. Without the ability to reduce excessive spending or modernize regulations, politicians will only delay major policy actions until they gain the leverage to do so. Such inaction has already impacted the market through arbitrary cuts to government programs and significant bureaucratic delays.[18]

Let Freedom Spend

In *Citizens United v. Federal Elections Commission* (2010), the Supreme Court ruled 5-4 that the money spent on campaigns by groups and individuals is protected under the First Amendment.[19] This means that companies, non-profit political groups, and unions are free to spend unlimited funds to indirectly support or oppose candidates during an election. Whether the Court correctly interpreted the Constitution is not the prime concern of this book, but it is essential to understand how the growth of election money ultimately feeds the political paralysis explained earlier.

The fears of exponential campaign spending were ultimately realized, when almost 4 billion dollars was spent on campaigns in 2012.[20] However, the end result of that spending has proven inconclusive. While many Republicans widely outspent their Democratic opponents, in close national races the Democrat ended up the victor. Hundreds of millions of dollars by outside groups could not stop the Obama campaign's political powerhouse, fueled by volunteers, small donations, and technological superiority. In terms of return on investment, several interest groups were extremely disappointed.[21]

The main concern regarding increased campaign spending is that it expands how money influences public policy. As more special interests become involved in the political scene, the pressure against making any changes that threaten these groups becomes even greater. This policy of favoritism disturbs the spirit of a competitive marketplace, which could significantly stifle innovation in these fields.

There has always been, and will always be, special interest groups who seek to influence the law in their favor. In fact, some of these advocacy organizations serve a vital function for public good. For instance, it took an alliance of academics and health experts to push for legislation on tobacco restrictions.[22] In addition, driving under the influence of alcohol was never a hot political issue until Mothers Against Drunk Driving (MADD) made it one.[23]

However, the prime source of stress for campaign reformers is not what has occurred, but what could occur. As the market for campaign ads and literature expands, the extreme amount of money spent will only worsen political gridlock. This threatens not only economic growth, but also the very essence of democratic capitalism. In addition, many business sectors would be compelled to participate in the political arena for fear of being overshadowed by their competitors.[24]

Concealed Culprits

There are many reasons for the great political antagonism. To get the best overview of our modern predicament, I would highly suggest purchasing, borrowing, or renting *It's Even Worse Than It Looks* by Thomas Mann and Norman Ornstein.[25] They provide an in-depth overview of the current political polarity, from the perspective of intellectuals from both sides of the spectrum. The solutions they suggest range from reasonable and viable to idealistic, but they are the best suggestions to date on how to fix this system. Some of my proposals are rooted in their writings.

To summarize their work, the ideological divide between the parties arose in part due to a variety of factors within the past half-century. Among these are: the growing presence of mass media, the increased conservative slant of the Republican Party (which has also pushed the Democrats to the left), and the greater concentration of money in politics. Each reason has slowly forced Congress to become incapable of enacting the necessary changes for our country to reach its full employment capacity.

Even though both parties play into partisan warfare, the truth is that the Republican Party is more responsible for the dysfunction we see in Congress today. This is *not* a vindication of conservative ideology or causes, as they have hardly anything to do with today's situation. Instead, the GOP has elected leaders who are increasingly ideological, and refuse to consider any practical measures or compromises that may give the Democrats any leverage.

Of course, Democrats are not innocent at this crime scene either. Their victories in 2006 and 2008 produced an overly optimistic atmosphere, and they believed that the voters gave them free reign to pursue a variety of progressive policies. As a result, they completely ignored many of the concerns for budgetary restraint. By disregarding the concern of conservative and moderate voters, they were overwhelmed when a sudden wave of Republican support led them to lose control of the House of Representatives.

This conservative resurgence is attributed to what is considered the Tea Party, a far-right bloc that adamantly insists on diminishing the role of government, especially when it comes to regulations. Despite its lackluster popularity amongst independents and moderates, it has maintained a substantial rate of success. This can be primarily attributed to a select few wealthy groups, which seek to promote their ideology by funding political action committees (PACs) that challenge more moderate Republicans.

This ideological divide between far-right politicians and more moderate leaders has created a split in the Republican Party. The same movement that propelled the GOP to victory in 2010 is now fighting for ideological control of the conservative brand. It is impossible to determine if their efforts will succeed in the short term, but it is safe to assume that political paralysis will remain strong as long as the Tea Party directs Republican politics. Democrats also suffer from intra-party conflict, but they are unified by a clear leadership structure as well as mutual disdain for conservative policy.

Another factor that has always played a strong role in political discourse is redistricting. Although the process of "gerrymandering" has been around since this nation's inception, new technologies and precise polling make it easy for legislators to carve a district that will remain politically predictable.[26] Constantly shifting districts make it difficult to remove incompetent or controversial politicians.

Currently, since there are more Republicans than Democrats in the House of Representatives, the Republican Party is in control. However, if you count the number of votes casted nationally during the 2012 election, more people voted for Democrats than Republicans.[27] If the United States followed a parliamentary system, where citizens vote for the party instead of the person, the Democrats would have full control of both chambers of Congress and the Presidency. While I do not advocate switching our representative system, this fact highlights how strong a role redistricting plays in maintaining incumbency.

Vote! Seriously, Vote!

Some economists argue that the value of voting is completely overstated, and that most people would better spend their time doing something productive rather than participating in an election.[28] Such claims completely ignore the hidden costs of letting the status quo continue, and focus more on the minor gains for consumers rather than the major costs of inadequate politicians.[29] In addition, political paralysis will contribute to diminished productivity in the market due to greater government inefficiency.[30] I only fear what would happen if gridlock prevented Congress from acting in the event of another market downturn.

I believe that it is economically vital to participate in local and national elections, to ensure that the leaders we choose are qualified and willing to work with their opponents. Thus, the single most important solution to the problems we have discussed in this chapter is to encourage voter participation and education. Democrats were successful in 2008 and 2012, and Republicans were successful in 2010, in part due to a surge in voter turnout by each respective party. Growing a moderate, independent voter base will send a signal to politicians to tone down their rhetoric, and could potentially encourage both parties to work with each other.[31]

We should also seek to expand access to the voting booth, so that individuals have a greater chance to cast their vote. Many countries with large populations hold elections on multiple days, to provide citizens several opportunities to vote at their convenience. The United States should follow suit by continuing to expand the early voting process for major elections.

Incumbents unfairly benefit from their power to dictate the rules and boundaries of elections. There is no strong argument in favor of allowing a majority party to redraw their own electoral maps, but arguments by citizens to mandate fair district borders have fallen on deaf ears. To guarantee balanced and competitive elections, campaign reformers have proposed to take the power of redistricting out of the hands of Congress and other legislatures, and put them into the hands of an independent body evenly split along party lines.

To address the issue of campaign spending, I endorse a constitutional amendment to reverse the *Citizens United* decision. Campaign spending is protected under the First Amendment, and there is nothing Congress or the president can do to reverse the trend of longer and more expensive elections. Amending the Constitution is incredibly difficult, and the prospects of this change occurring anytime soon are rather dim. However, there is growing momentum amongst concerned voters, businesses, and politicians who are disgusted by the current political climate, and the arguments against the status quo are becoming increasingly baseless.

Politicians may not steer the capitalist ship, but their actions affect the course of its trajectory. Liberals and conservatives will always argue over the role government should play in steering our economy, but we have rarely seen a time where such disagreements stalled productivity and growth. Greater political paralysis has made it more difficult to control the rudder, and it could prevent our vessel from making necessary turns to avoid dangerous obstacles. By making crucial repairs, we can more effectively avoid further threats to our ship, and allow it to accelerate towards long-term growth.

*LeadAmerica was later acquired by Envision EMI in 2012.

Chapter 5

Unemployment

George Segal's *Breadline Sculpture* at the Franklin Delano Roosevelt Memorial in Washington, DC, February 24, 2010

AT FIRST GLANCE, having the unemployment rate (released by the Bureau of Labor Statistics) be anything above zero percent would seem to be a symptom of an underperforming economy. For economists, however, having unemployment below a certain level is actually a bad sign. During prosperous times, there are instances when people decide to leave their job. Whether the purpose of departure is to start a new business or escape an unsuitable workplace, having the flexibility to enter and leave the job market is essential to a thriving marketplace. Without this permeable barrier between employment and unemployment, people are forced to work in long-term positions that do not maximize their skill sets, reducing production and potential growth. Most experts aim for an average rate of unemployment that hovers around 4-5% of the active labor pool.[1]

Economists, policymakers, and businesses love to throw around the term "full employment." This phrase is the catch-all definition of an economy that operates at full capacity. Everyone capable of working is able to find a job, and businesses are in the best position to produce new products and create innovative technologies.[2] The marketplace seeks to achieve this state of business nirvana, which promises the greatest output and income for all participants.

However, today's employment situation is anything but ideal, as many individuals are unable to obtain a suitable job. The worst result of the most recent recession is the destruction of millions of mid-level salaried positions, decimating entire sectors or forcing them to scale back.[3] Since the downturn began, the puzzle to restore the economy to pre-recession levels has almost been completed. The financial sector has returned to normal operations and job openings are increasing, as businesses are no longer afraid to hire new workers. However, solving the issue of high unemployment and underemployment remains the missing piece of the puzzle.

The topic of employment (specifically, the lack thereof) is the prime focus of this chapter. For the past five years, the unemployment rate has fallen from its height of 10%, but remains substantially higher than economists prefer.[4] We face a serious dilemma regarding the future of employment, one that could severely hinder our status as an economic power. Finding a solution will be the greatest challenge of this generation, as the long-term unemployed will be a significant resource drain in the coming decades.

Who are the Unemployed?

Before we can find a solution to the unemployment problem, it is essential to first understand the demographics of the new jobless Americans. As of March 2014, there are currently approximately 10 million people who are currently considered unemployed by the Department of Labor's Bureau of Labor Statistics (BLS).[5] These are individuals who are looking for work, but have been unable to find employment within the past month. However, there are unofficial estimates that place the number of unemployed much higher, because they have either given up looking for work until the economy improves or are unable to qualify for unemployment benefits. The official estimates from the BLS indicate that around 12% of all potential laborers have not found work.[6]

Approximately 16% of young individuals (15-24 year olds) who are able to participate in the workforce have been unable to find a job.[7] This is partially due to a hyper-competitive employment market, with college graduates competing with older individuals that have far more experience. Because of this, many younger individuals are furthering their education while waiting for jobs to open up.

While young people make up a significant percentage of the unemployed, middle-aged or older individuals without work are a greater concern. As stated earlier, the recession led to millions of people getting laid off, with the construction and manufacturing sectors suffering the greatest.[8] Many of these individuals are only equipped with a high school education, rely on outdated skill sets, or were replaced by younger and more active workers.[9] It is increasingly difficult for this generation of workers to find a job that matches their prior compensation.

The most recent recession has been harsh for lower-skilled and undereducated workers. Many middle class positions were eliminated, and the only available substitutes for these individuals are low-wage jobs.[10] In addition, one surprising development that has economists deeply concerned is the above average number of unemployed or underemployed well-educated laborers.[11] A college degree alone is no longer a guarantee for a stable job, and many jobs being filled by recent graduates offer pay that is far below what they deserve.

Lost in Occupation Translation

The first question to answer is how unemployment can remain stubbornly high while almost all other economic indicators show strong growth. The prime reason is that millions of able-bodied workers were laid off, and the jobs they held disappeared as the recession played out. This means that many lower and middle class Americans can no longer find jobs in their trained field, leaving them unable to find a replacement position.

There were almost 4 million job openings in the United States at the end of 2013.[12] While this seems encouraging at face value, it is important to understand what these occupations entail. Many of the job openings available require a high level of technical expertise, or are in fields where the majority of the unemployed have no experience. Most of the lower-skilled jobs have either been shipped overseas or pay wages significantly below what the new unemployed were given at their previous workplace.

There is also the issue of regional disparities, as the cities or states that have the highest job growth do not correspond to the population as a whole.[13] There are significant barriers for a middle-income family to move to a new location, such as proximity to relatives and friends, high housing prices, and a lack of necessary connections. The housing crash exacerbates this problem, as most people who want to move cannot pay off their mortgage or would be forced to sell their home at a lower price than they initially purchased it at.

There is also the problem of compensation and educational inequality. The number of moderate-wage jobs that require a high-school degree or less are steadily decreasing, which disqualifies over a third of all unemployed Americans from finding an adequately paid position.[14] Instead, minimum wage and part-time work is one of the fastest growing options available for these individuals.

The higher salaried jobs require a significant educational investment, either through formal college learning, vocational training, or certification. All of these options are becoming increasingly expensive, as the demand for higher learning rises without any informal price controls. In addition, companies are reluctant to invest in training for new employees, and instead seek to maximize the labor of their current staff.

Government jobs appear to have weathered the worst effects of the recession.[15] Since there is always a need for government services and institutions, the federal and state bureaucracy has long been held as a safe haven from market downturns. Unfortunately, due to cuts by state legislatures, even low-level government workers are under constant threat of losing their jobs. Concerns about the deficit have lead to further cuts by the federal government, which has experienced a slowdown in hiring for administrative positions.

Generation Degradation

The growing inequality in job compensation threatens the mobility that originally inspired millions of immigrants to move to the United States. If there is little hope for foreign workers or their children to obtain a decent paying job in this country, then there is little reason for them to move here. This is a dangerous trend, as inequality in compensation will inevitably lead to growing income disparity. This results in a stagnant or lower standard of living for the vast majority of Americans, encouraging income inequality and undermining the economy as a whole.

As extended unemployment benefits expire, many older individuals are resorting to temporary measures to maintain their livelihood. Most will likely take part-time or temporary jobs to make ends meet.[16] Others will sell prized or valuable possessions to earn money until their job prospects improve.*

There are major consequences for letting older individuals fend for themselves. First, there will be a significant increase in expenditures by the government and other individuals to care for them. While these funds could have a temporary stimulating effect on the market, they do not result in any significant increases in labor productivity. In other words, the economy cannot grow further without having this income being tied to some form of work.

There is nothing inherently wrong with giving money to people who cannot find work. However, we must recognize that the fiscal reality of high middle-age unemployment reduces our capacity to do so. A significant portion of the US government's revenue is derived from income taxes.[17] If a sizable percentage of older individuals are no longer working, the obvious result is lower revenues to care for them when they retire.

This problem is exaggerated by the fact that the upcoming retirees are the largest generation in US history (Baby Boomers, or people born between 1946-1964). This segment of the population expects a level of entitlement when they have not provided their proportional share.[18] Without employing more of the Baby Boom generation, the government will have no choice but to cut back programs that care for the elderly and disabled, or cease them entirely.

When it comes to income and benefits, young individuals have been dealt a worse hand than their parents and grandparents. The millennial generation has appropriately responded to the demand for more educated workers by going to college en masse. However, the greater emphasis on higher learning has lead to unprecedented levels of tuition increases.[19] In addition, the higher costs of attending a university has not produced a similar return on investment for a large segment of graduates. Many students lucky enough to receive an entry-level position in their field will be forced to deal with a tremendous amount of debt.

It is essential to consider how the unemployment problem affects the occupational mobility of younger workers. Because many new jobs are outside the expertise many young individuals are trained in, they require more time and education to be able to partake in greater opportunities. However, the rising debt that is burdened by this generation is limiting the capacity to obtain these resources, leaving them stuck with an unemployable skill set.[20]

Blame the Intern

Another trend worth considering is the rise of internships, both unpaid and paid. Internships are intended to provide real-world experience for young individuals, without requiring a significant investment on the part of the participating organization. In theory, this form of employment should offer direct experience for newcomers to the professional world, and improve the prospects for a future job in the same line of work.

However, there are rising concerns that internships are actually harming the labor market. As the labor market remains unstable, young individuals are desperate to earn noteworthy experience. As a result, there is intense competition for internships, despite the lack of pay or earned college credit. In addition, businesses have been increasingly reliant upon interns for basic functions, eliminating many entry-level positions that, at one time, signified a stepping-stone for paid employment.[21]

Students are encouraged to spend a year or more committed to unpaid work to be hired in a well-paid position. Not only does this increase the growing debt many students will face, but also automatically disqualifies poorer individuals from partaking in this necessary step. As a result, the inequality in training and valuable work experience between wealthy and lower class individuals will rise unsustainably. This threatens socioeconomic mobility, and poses a serious threat to middle class households.

Currently, unpaid internships are considered legal if they are for the exclusive benefit of the intern, not the company.** However, beyond this, anything is permissible, including hourly requirements, compensation below minimum wage and sexual harassment.[22] There is also no enforcement of the standards established and no incentive for the intern to call out against abuse. Doing so nullifies any work experience from the offending company, and raises red flags against further employment prospects.

Unfortunately, there is no strong reasonable advocacy on behalf of this increasingly exploited group. There are organizations that seek justice for abused interns, but they usually advocate for the elimination of the practice outright. I argue against this, as unpaid internships provide crucial experience that many employers are increasingly looking for.[23] Instead, I encourage pushing for laws that extend most legal protections employees have to interns, while preserving the capacity for businesses to host unpaid internships.

Creative Policy Counters Creative Destruction

There are many policy proposals that aim to improve the unemployment situation. Most of the repairs to the labor market will come from private companies and organizations, but governments can speed up the process through programs that directly address the core causes of chronic unemployment. There is no clear path out of this mess, but the following proposals are the best options I have come up with to prevent future economic calamities.

The most basic and straightforward answer to our dilemma is to greatly expand free or inexpensive occupational training programs. The government will most likely spearhead the majority of these programs, but non-profit organizations and businesses can also play a key role in creating a newly educated workforce. The advantage of this proposal is that it directly tackles the issue of chronic unemployment amongst older workers. This group needs highly technical skills for new economic times, and giving them an inexpensive means of doing so will increase their output potential.

Unfortunately, many governments are in a state of contraction, and providing revenue for these programs is increasingly difficult. Even though growing deficits are a legitimate concern, not addressing the problem of high unemployment will create a state of fiscal instability that no government finds desirable. To remedy both the problem of deficits and unemployment, governments could *temporarily* raise taxes by modest levels for higher income individuals to specifically fund these programs. Alternatively, they could enact tax exemptions for companies and individuals that host or sponsor them. The advantage of this proposal is that, if implemented effectively, it will likely pay for itself, as lost revenue is made up through more spending and taxable income from newly employed consumers.

An idea that goes hand-in-hand with job programs for adults is what is known as STEM (Science, Technology, Engineering, and Math) programs. As the booming technology sector promises a strong bounty for anyone who partakes in it, schools and policymakers are increasingly focusing on subjects relevant to the new economy. STEM programs are promising in that they are directly training students in fields that will play a prominent role in the 21st century.[24] The emphasis on technology is also providing schools with much-needed funds to replace outdated computers, books, and teaching tools.

I endorse STEM programs for their potential to equip students with skills necessary for the modern job market, but caution against implementing these programs haphazardly. Although the subjects emphasized are especially important for employment, they alone cannot guarantee employability. Students should also have a keen understanding of the visual and performing arts, reading, writing, and the social sciences. We should not prohibit them from exploring subjects that interest them due to lower funds for non-STEM classes.

We have thus far talked about fixing the unemployment crisis with the current labor pool in mind, but have not adequately addressed proposals aimed toward promoting businesses that hire. There are already benefits for companies that hire new workers in the US, but these policies should go a few steps further. The government needs to provide additional relief for companies that train their workers for skills essential to the modern economy. This proposal addresses the problem of high unemployment for younger and older individuals, as it allows both groups to earn employable skills while earning necessary income.

In order for this program or incentive to work, it must be carefully constructed to avoid potential abuse by businesses or employees. Setting the benefits too high could lead to businesses immediately firing their new recruits once they finish, while lower benefits would make these programs cost prohibitive for smaller businesses. In addition, these programs should be properly regulated and surveyed, as the potential for workplace abuse is high where the employee is entirely dependent on the training to stay in the workforce. On the receiving end, workers are obliged to foster productivity in the company they are trained under. There is also an expectation of good performance, which is entirely dependent on the work ethic of the new employee.

The need for adequate protections for unpaid and paid interns is essential to improving the labor market. As companies and organizations increasingly rely upon interns for the company's daily functions, these individuals must have laws that back them against abusive business practices. The best way to achieve this is through legal action or legislation at the federal level. At the very least, such actions will slow or halt the trend of transforming interns into a source of free labor.

The Great American Back Scratch

I write this book as someone who is incredibly lucky, and has the system "rigged" on his behalf. I entered college almost immediately after the recession officially ended, and intentionally obtained skills that would allow me to find a job suitable to my interests or studied field. Though I am grateful for my situation, I cannot be comfortable knowing that many in this country face dismal employment prospects. My motivation for highlighting our unemployment problem stems from a desire to avoid impending economic disasters that threaten this country.

Our economy cannot succeed with an attitude of self-servitude, and those who achieved the greatest success must provide for those whose opportunities were swept away due to forces beyond their control. Unless there is a strong push on behalf of potential job seekers, we will continue to face the consequences of lost productivity. We can avoid the worst of this storm by acting today to help the unemployed find suitable jobs.

Secondhand sales are not included as part of the GDP, as no new goods are being produced. Thus, this is not the option most economists would prefer.

I feel the need to disclose that I have had many internships at various organizations, none of which I considered exploitive.

Chapter 6

Education

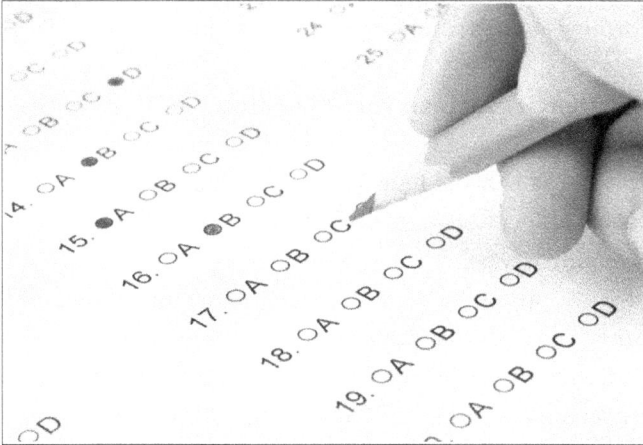

Multiple-choice test

ONE OF PRESIDENT GEORGE W. BUSH'S most recognizable actions is the implementation of the No Child Left Behind (NCLB) program. This initiative was originally intended to improve the education standards across the country, particularly in regions with the lowest performing school districts. NCLB received bipartisan support when it was passed by Congress in 2002, and was seen as a promising step that would address many of the problems plaguing our learning institutions.[1]

The main emphasis of the law was on school performance, and attempted to tie financial incentives for at-risk schools and districts to improve their test scores. By allowing each state to set their own goals and standards for greater student performance, they are better able to evaluate how each school is faring. What lawmakers assumed would happen would be that structural failures within the public education system would be corrected, by ensuring teacher accountability and adequate materials for each student.

Unfortunately, it was not long before problems and controversies began to emerge. Many teachers complained that their curriculum needed to be modified to only cover what would be tested.[2] In addition, there were many implicit attempts by many states to lower academic standards in order to improve test scores.[3] In addition, although the law was intended to service minority or impoverished students, these children continued to suffer from a considerable performance gap compared to their well-off counterparts.[4]

This chapter examines the prime challenges our education system faces, and the long-run impact these problems will have on our economy. The single greatest investment a person can make to improve his or her productivity and livelihood is obtaining quality education. As a result, it is in the best interest of businesses, households, and governments to maintain our learning institutions. However, the recession and other factors have created incredible roadblocks that make it difficult to provide adequate education for all students.

Although the United States has several of the best learning institutions in the world, many schools across the nation do not provide their students with the skills necessary to compete in the marketplace. To maintain our status as an economic superpower, we must ensure that future generations have an educational background that allows for flexibility in the job market. This will require many changes, both in the structure of our school system and the way we think about learning. With rapid developments in technology and information sharing, now is the best time to consider re-writing the textbook on the best models for learning.

Education is a controversial subject in economic and political discussions. Parents, teachers, administrators, policymakers, businesses, and students have very strong opinions regarding the most efficient and productive means to improve this "broken" system. I will attempt to avoid favoring any particular group or campaign, and it is essential to critically examine the proposals of each side on key issues. However, the goal of this book is not to guarantee victory or defeat for certain players, but to fix chronic impediments to ensure that each student has an equal opportunity to obtain a baseline education.

All Children are Above Average

A high school education, which provides essential knowledge of mathematics, language, art, history, and other important topics, was long considered the baseline requirement for middle class employment. By giving every citizen the opportunity to receive a high school diploma, our society ensured that all new workers would be qualified for a vast array of jobs. College and other supplementary education was reserved only for those who were either wealthy or dedicated enough to pursue work that required further training and knowledge.

Unfortunately, the recent recession has made it abundantly clear that a high school diploma is no longer adequate for most middle-income positions. The unemployment rate for high school graduates is slightly above the national average.[5] Businesses that hire high school graduates typically offer low-wage or part-time work, which barely amounts to a middle class income. Though the recession is mostly to blame for this situation, there are no signs of relief as the economy continues its sluggish recovery.

Solving this dilemma requires a thorough examination of the job market itself, as well as an understanding of what a high school education stands for. Until recently, a high school diploma served as a symbol of competent work, as anyone who works and studies hard enough is capable of receiving one. Companies hired these graduates under the assumption that they would be easy to train and can handle the stress of the modern world. However, as labor costs increased and shipping costs dropped significantly, many corporations sent low-skill jobs overseas.

Simultaneously, the apparent value of a high school diploma has dropped, as more middle and upper-income jobs require at least a college degree. Though all high school graduates are capable of understanding basic math and linguistics, the technical skills most companies seek are not included in the curriculum of our education system. To make matters worse, the recent recession has forced many college-educated workers to seek positions previously filled by those without a bachelor's degree. This intense competition results in companies hiring those with more training and experience, pushing high school diploma recipients to a lower socioeconomic status.

These changes have encouraged students to attempt to receive a college education. While this is a worthwhile endeavor for those seeking to specialize in a particular field, there are many students who are pressured to attend a university for fear of being disqualified from the job market. Due to the rapid rise in demand for higher learning, many academic institutions have greatly increased their tuition costs. This threatens to bar many lower-income students from obtaining a college degree, trapping them in a perpetual spiral of chronic poverty.

Policymakers, especially President Obama, have focused primarily on increasing access to a college education.[6] However, if they truly intend to help all Americans in the modern labor market, the first step should be to greatly increase the value of a high school education. Such an endeavor will not be easy or popular, and there are strong political repercussions for those who anger key educational groups.

Teach a Man to Maximize Productivity

A proper high school curriculum should cover a wide range of subjects, all of which we would consider essential for a well-rounded individual. However, the time a student spends in primary and secondary school is highly restricted, and there is intense competition between academic fields to have higher priority over others. As a result, the school curriculum in many districts is stretched thin to cover these subjects in a limited time frame.

The most recent initiative to modernize our education system involves placing greater emphasis on STEM (Science, Technology, Engineering, Math) courses and magnet programs.[7] The employment prospects in technological and scientific sectors are promising, but there is insufficient coverage of these subjects in most high schools. While there are institutions that offer these subjects, they are not mandatory for graduation, signaling that a high school diploma does not prepare students for the real world.

The process of transforming our schools to include a greater emphasis on STEM programs has been slow, but promising. However, it is important to remember that students should also have ample time to expand their horizons in other academic fields. We cannot ignore that a basic understanding of the fine arts, literature, physical exercise, and other subjects are crucial to our national culture.

While we take steps to improve our high schools, there should also be an effort to better prepare students who seek post-secondary education. In the final years of attendance, students should be provided resources and information to prepare them for college. In addition, local employers should have the opportunity to recruit new workers directly from the high school itself, and should collaborate with schools to develop training programs for graduates.

Learning Permit

Thus far, we have focused considerably on the structure of effective education policy and curriculums. While these steps are essential to reform our school system, none of these changes will matter unless we also examine the teaching process and institutions as well. The largest portion of total education spending is applied toward the salaries of instructors, who have a tremendous impact on the success of their students.[8]

Teachers are the ground troops in our education system, and should be provided the necessary training and compensation to effectively instruct our students. By interacting with these children on a regular basis, an educator can identify problems that would otherwise go unnoticed by parents or local authorities.[9] A well-regarded teacher is also able to compensate for flaws in our educational system by making efficient use of the resources he or she has available.

The idea that our education system is faulty because too many bad teachers infiltrate the system is an exaggeration. Outside of the university system, educators are paid middle-of-the-road salaries, with little room for growth other than cost of living adjustments.[10] The main incentive for these individuals is to provide a service to future generations. Without that drive, the work necessary to be an instructor is a grueling exercise in redundancy.

Part of the problem with the debate over effective versus ineffective teachers is that there is no practical way to measure instructional performance uniformly.[11] Standardized testing is the most direct means of evaluation, but cannot account for external factors such as poverty or mental illness. In addition, because each academic subject is different from one another, it is difficult to determine teacher performance. This would require a complete analysis of each individual academic department, and it is costly and complex to develop flexible standards.

Literally Old School

Another concern many education reformers have is the operating status of our schools. Without proper funding or regulations, these institutions are unable to meet state or federal guidelines, creating a bureaucratic nightmare. For instance, poor sanitization or sub-par building conditions are a major inhibitor of student performance.[12] On a related note, children who attend schools near facilities that produce environmental hazards may experience chronic exposure to toxic chemicals, which damages their health and potential academic achievement.[13]

Many schools are forced to rely on outdated or insufficient technologies, which prevents them from teaching essential computer skills necessary for the modern labor market.[14] The cost of accessing educational materials has significantly declined due to technological advancements. However, many teachers and administrators fail to take advantage of them due to insufficient training in their use.[15] While this problem is diminishing as computers become omnipresent in our society, schools are slow to integrate digital devices as instructional aids.

One topic that warrants further discussion is the structure of the modern classroom. The model of a single teacher lecturing a room full of students will always be a cost-effective method of learning. However, ensuring every child's success requires tailoring homework and assistance to each individual's needs. There are many prototype programs, mainly in large urban areas such as New York City, which do away with the traditional classroom and instead provide technological tools to help students learn at their own pace.[16]

The development of virtual classes and online tutoring has opened up a new frontier for education. With proper supervision, a student is just as capable of learning concepts using what is provided online as he or she is in a normal classroom. The advantage of using such systems is that they are more cost-efficient, giving children living in lower-income households the opportunity to obtain high quality education.[17]

It is unlikely that online education will supplement physical schools, and teachers will still play a vital role in helping a child learn.[18] However, the best way to reduce the education gap is to ensure everyone has access to effective learning tools. It will take a few decades before these developments are adapted as standard practice, but we should ultimately be open to the possibility of using technology to teach and assist in ways the standard classroom model cannot.

Home Work

The environment and culture outside of school is just as important, if not more so, as the conditions of the academic facilities themselves. Even if a child attends the best academic institutions, they cannot provide shelter from lackluster conditions at home. That is why poverty is widely considered to be a significant hindrance to success in school, and addressing it will greatly improve a student's prospects.[19]

Almost every education expert and advocate stresses the importance of a parent's involvement in a child's academic success. As a result, it is easy for policymakers to blame poor performance or behavior on the part of "bad parents" who do not care enough for their child. Because of this, our education system has been set up in such a way that places too much emphasis on punishment rather than assistance.[20]

However, such an image hides the miserable conditions these households face, many of which are run by single mothers who work full-time jobs.[21] The average middle class family usually has at least one parent who is capable of helping and supervising his or her child. On the other hand, lower-income households typically have one or both parents working long and late hours, leaving little time for them to interact.

Young individuals living in impoverished communities are distracted by the conditions they live in, and are more likely to be exposed to criminal elements.[22] In addition, adult supervision of children is much less common in these areas, resulting in less pressure for them to complete their schoolwork. Most deviant behavior arises from students in unstable households, which is why punishing them with suspension often has little effect.

There are non-profit and government programs that seek to aid students living in adverse conditions. Many children can rely on certain after-school programs and safe havens for study and play without worrying about food and shelter. However, until city and state governments address the poverty in their dominion, the success of these programs will continue to be muted.

Public Service Denouncement

There have been significant developments over the past few years that will have a tremendous impact on education standards and performance. As public schools continue to suffer from a variety of problems, private institutions have attempted to fill in the void. The number of private "charter" academies has increased considerably, and a greater proportion of public education funding is being devoted to increasing enrollment rates for these establishments.[23]

There is nothing inherently wrong with allowing the growth of private education. The purpose of sending a student to these schools is to provide him or her with excellent learning opportunities, which may be underdeveloped in local public schools. Parents seek the best education for their children, and they are willing to pay a premium if the top schools are outside of the public sphere.

Unfortunately, the movement of sending children toward private education is actually undermining our public education system as a whole. The assumption that these institutions are completely separate from the public schooling system or self-sustaining is false. Many of these institutions are run by for-profit groups, and seek to maximize revenue, relying increasingly on state and local governments funds.[24] This creates a scenario where money, teachers, and other resources are being drained away from public schools in favor of private academic facilities. Many children from lower-income families are unable to access or afford enrollment at these schools, and are saddled with an increasingly stressed public education sector.

To counteract the potential of marginalizing impoverished households, private education advocates have pushed for government-sponsored vouchers that allow poor children to attend top-tier schools.[25] This policy makes sense from a local level, but implementing it on a larger scale creates enormous challenges in the long run. While the students who receive these vouchers can experience better educational opportunities, those who either do not receive them or qualify for them will be trapped in poorly performing schools. Not only do vouchers completely ignore the problems that cause academic systems to fail, but they also fuel the achievement gap and income inequality as a whole.[26]

Of course, the entire argument in favor of private schooling rests on the assumption that it will always remain superior to public education, because they follow market principles such as competition. While this supposedly encourages innovation and creative thinking, it also automatically creates winners and losers. The private schools that perform the poorest relative to their competitors are likely to see their funds quickly dry up, and the students attending these institutions are likely to either see a significant drop in the quality of their education or will be forced to transfer to another school entirely. Such instability is dangerous, and does not offer the best return on investment for the state and local governments sponsoring these schools.

Even if all students were to transfer to these private institutions, the problems endemic to the education system would still not be addressed in full. Young individuals living in poverty would still face numerous obstacles that would distract them from academic success. In addition, these schools do nothing to improve the value of a high school degree, or help mitigate the costs of a college education.

Reformers and policymakers should focus first and foremost on improving public school districts before they seek to push private learning any further. Unless the problems plaguing the education system are addressed, we will continue to see few improvements from this trend. Once these issues are corrected or mitigated, it will then be appropriate to consider boosting private competition.

Common Core-tesy

The other recent change is the rise of the Common Core State Standards (also known as Common Core), a benchmark for academic achievement. This state-based initiative has been discussed at great length in public and academic circles, and has ignited fierce controversy with regards to its implementation.[27] Most of this fervor is based on misleading information, originating both from advocates and opponents. To understand the economic impact of such a program, it is essential to understand what exactly Common Core is and what its implications are for education.

Until the mid-20th century, education was considered a mostly local domain, teaching only what the community required to participate as a functioning adult. However, as globalization greatly increased the need for an educated workforce, unified standards arose across the country. Common Core has many predecessors, but it is one of the first initiatives to start at the national level and trickle down to the states.

Education standards guarantee that students are learning at a modest but efficient pace, with little overlap or gaps in curriculum. Currently, the only set of standards Common Core has is in K-12 Math and English, but there are many plans to expand into other academic subjects.[28] While most states have adopted these standards, they are able to adjust them without any major consequences.

While there is nothing alarming about this development at first, the concerns regarding the implementation and standards set up by the Common Core are somewhat legitimate. If states tie a substantial portion of funds to Common Core testing, the end result is inevitably a curriculum that only focuses on those standards. In addition, the Common Core has yet to be adequately tested on an experimental level, and may not impact student performance.[29]

In addition, the push to adopt Common Core arises from private companies that provide educational resources, leading many to assume that this initiative is largely a profit venture for these entities.[30] New curriculums require a significant investment on the part of school districts, and there is no guarantee that states implementing Common Core will also include funds to obtain necessary materials. Online resources can provide inexpensive and easily accessible learning exercises for students and teachers, but there has been no mention of providing such resources under these guidelines. The only option for schools that have insufficient funds is to either raise taxes or cut costs significantly in other subjects.

Despite these concerns, I would not dismiss or demolish the Common Core as a whole. The value of a high school education should resemble a baseline of adequate knowledge, and should be almost equal when traveling from state-to-state. The fears of a federal takeover of education policy are exaggerated and unsophisticated, as opposing unified standards do nothing to improve the quality of education itself. Instead, the states and federal government should include the input of education experts, teachers, parents, and school administrators when developing these guidelines.

Good Policy = Good Schools

Reforming and improving our education system is an important measure for economists, as it provides the means to improve productivity in the market as a whole. The days where low-skilled labor can be paid at middle class wages is slowly coming to an end, and most new jobs require an extensive academic background. The current economic recovery provides an excellent opportunity to implement policies and changes that fundamentally raise the performance of our students.

The current Secretary of Education, Arne Duncan, stresses that the countries ranked highest in education are more likely to have a system where incentives are set up for teachers, students, and schools to perform well.[31] We should take this message as a mandate to find the best educational approaches and reward innovations in teaching. The "Race to the Top" program, which allows states and school districts to compete for funding through innovative changes, is an advancement of the traditional method of tying academic performance to financial reward.

The next generation of educators should be proficiently trained, and the measures taken to become a teacher should be competitive and challenging. Groups such as Teach For America actively recruit academically trained students straight out of college, ensuring that all candidates for a teaching position have at least a bachelor's degree in the subject they teach.[32] To accommodate these highly qualified educators, school districts should properly compensate these teachers to attract the best educators.

Education is intended to prepare students for the demands of the modern workplace. Technology is becoming an essential part of a young individual's life, and there should be no reason to assume that schools are incapable of integrating this fact into their curriculum. A top priority for school districts is to make certain that computer literacy and other modern skills are integrated into the curriculum, and that educators have the proper materials to teach these classes.

Technological innovation has made it easier and cheaper to provide effective resources for students to learn. Local or state governments should encourage using these tools by providing incentives for teachers using new or updated mediums to teach. In addition, policies should be put in place that propose tax benefits for tech companies that offer their products for educators at reduced prices.

As I stated earlier, it is important for education reformers to primarily focus on improving public schools before attempting to increase enrollment in private institutions. The current trend toward funding private over public education must be reversed to provide public schools more flexibility to enact necessary changes. In the meantime, it may be useful for education experts to study high-performance private schools to see what can be passed on to public schools at a lower cost.

I would briefly like to address another form of institutional learning known as Montessori schools. The students at these institutions, rather than follow a rigid curriculum, learn at their own pace with the supervision and guidance of their teachers. This method is considered a less restrictive means of educating young individuals, and the schools that follow this model are quickly growing in popularity.[33] Although these programs have seen tremendous success, it is too early to consider implementing this model nationwide. Still, it is worth studying how these schools function, and if their practices can be applied in schools located in at-risk neighborhoods.

The United States falls behind other nations when it comes to education standards, but there are several steps that we can take to improve our rank. The most straightforward recommendation from these countries is to lengthen the time spent in primary and secondary schools. This can either occur through extending the overall school year, or by increasing the length of the average school day. While these proposals are not likely to be popular (particularly amongst children), they represent a significant commitment towards having the best-educated workforce.

This chapter predominantly focused on improving the secondary education level and below. However, there should also be efforts to increase accessibility to college or other professional training. High schools, as well as state and local governments, should provide resources and financial planning to help students to afford a university education. In addition, online establishments such as Coursera and Lynda offer promise in providing more technical skills to the average individual.

When traveling on a long and complex voyage, it is essential to have a crew with experience and nautical knowledge before setting off in dangerous waters. Without an adequately educated middle class, the capitalist ship risks having its sails deteriorate, causing the vessel to slow down in the long run. The time to fix this threat is running short, as these problems will become more difficult and expensive to address. Solving our education conundrum will allow us to maintain the integrity of our ship, and avoid other obstacles on our journey.

Chapter 7

Health Care

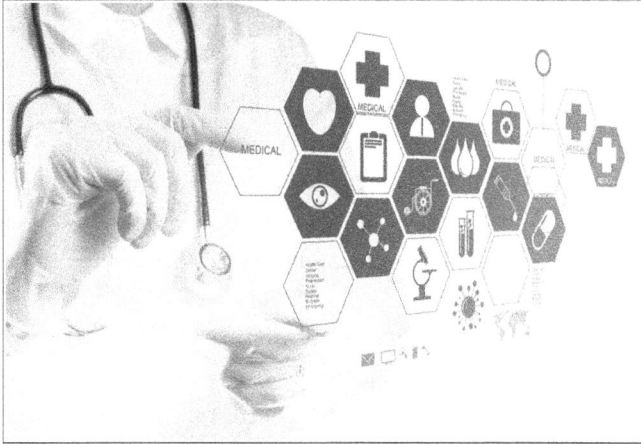

"May I never see in the patient anything but a fellow creature in pain."

- Oath of Maimonides

DURING THE 1940S, WORLD WAR II ERA policies prohibited employers from paying substantial incomes.[1] Without higher wages, some businesses needed incentives to attract highly desirable employees. Eventually, companies began offering health insurance as a benefit to entice qualified candidates to work for them. Over time, the wage ceiling was removed, but businesses continued to offer health insurance benefits to their workers.

At the time, the price employers had to pay to offer such benefits was rather minimal. However, modern companies are finding themselves with incredibly high insurance bills as the cost of health care rises exponentially.[2] What was once a benefit for upper-level positions has expanded to almost every full-time worker in the United States, making it difficult to hire new employees. If medical expenses continue to rise at a substantially higher rate than inflation, companies may be forced to reduce their staff to save costs.

It is not only businesses that are faced with uncomfortable decisions regarding health care. Doctors are increasingly aware of the expense certain procedures cost, and must make decisions based not only on a particular patient's health, but also his or her finances. Physicians took an oath like the one above when they graduated medical school, but are finding it harder to comply with their duties as a healer.

This chapter covers health care, and all the challenges associated with modern medicine. The cost of treatment continues to rise at a rapid rate, with only modest signs of slowing down. The World Bank estimates that medical services accounted for almost 18% of the total US GDP expenditures, a number that is only set to increase.[3] The United States hosts many of the best doctors and innovative treatments in the world, and is the epicenter for groundbreaking medical research. However, we lag behind most other developed countries in terms of the quality of health care for the average citizen, and the overall costs are far above the norm throughout the globe.[4]

I will explain why costs continue to rise, as well as the faults of applying traditional economic theory to an industry that literally determines life or death. Since there is a severe misunderstanding behind the Affordable Care Act (also known as "Obamacare"), I will also briefly describe how this law attempts to improve the market, and why such a feat may prove difficult. There are many proposed solutions and alternative systems to our current dilemma, and I will examine how effective and realistic they can be.

It is safe to say that the medical industry is about to embark on a massive transformation. I believe that we can overcome the challenges plaguing the health care system, but it will require time and a great deal of sacrifice from all parties involved. The health care industry will never magically become cheaper while simultaneously more accessible, but by applying economic principles it is possible to maximize the care a patient receives.

Save Lives, Earn Money, Repeat

It is strange how one of the most important industries in the American economy is also the most paradoxical, as it does not follow many of the normal customs of the marketplace. The laws of supply and demand, which normally dictate the prices and quantity of goods and services sold, do not lead to stable and consistent health care costs. The reason for this dilemma is that the demand for medical care is extremely high, and does not discourage providers to charge higher rates for their services.[5] In addition, competition in the health care sector is not adequate enough to reduce costs, as most regions across the nation have only one or two hospitals within a reasonable distance from a community.

One of the prime reasons that the medical sector is such an anomaly is that the method of paying for this service is vastly different from any other. Most goods and services are either paid for immediately by the individual, or deferred to a later point via direct billing. The price for these transactions is usually set in stone, with little room to negotiate a lower price. However, most Americans have health insurance, and the insurance company (or the government if you have Medicare or Medicaid) negotiates with the care center for a lower price. They pay all or a significant portion of that bill, and the insured individual pays whatever fees remain according to their insurance coverage.

What most people do not realize is that the discount that insurance companies receive is usually under half of the original cost. The unfortunate effect of lower payments is that hospitals compensate by greatly raising their prices, under the assumption that the insurance companies will ask for a lower percentage of that (highly inflated) number. However, insurance companies have gradually attempted to pay less for procedures, leading to an endless cycle of rising prices and greater discounts.[6] The ultimate loser is the average uninsured individual, who must pay the full retail price for these treatments.

The best medicine and procedural options have always been considered a luxury good, but the rate at which health care is changing is so rapid that it is impossible for the market to properly adjust. Hospitals and other care providers try to use the most up-to-date technologies and diagnostic equipment, which is an expensive investment from the start.[7] However, innovations in the medical field can occur within just a few years. These institutions are pressured to make significant profits from the technology they currently have so they can cover the costs of continuously upgrading their equipment.

For most other services purchased, the consumer is able to research prices in advance, or at least receive a ballpark estimate. However, when it comes to health care, the costs of one procedure can vary greatly from hospital to hospital. Oftentimes, the consumer is unable to know the full cost of their care in advance. Until recently, the price of common procedures remained known only to medical practitioners and insurance companies, leaving the patient in the dark.[8] Emergency treatment further complicates this scenario, as the patient usually has no choice as to where they are treated, and may end up burdened with tens of thousands of dollars in medical expenses.

Money is a Potent Drug

We have come a long way from the days of ineffective practices such as bloodletting and healing rituals. Diseases such as whooping cough and cholera have been suppressed or eliminated thanks to scientific research. The companies and institutions that answer the "call to cure" invest a significant amount of money and labor. These businesses have been the driving force behind the rapid pace of medical advancement.

The major growth of the pharmaceutical industry has proven to be a great catalyst for innovation. Companies such as Pfizer, Abbott, and Merck, whose brand medications cover a wide range of diseases, developed many drugs, vaccines, and other medical tools used today. Outside of good intentions, there is also a substantial profit incentive for these groups to fund research that will likely lead to cures for major diseases.[9]

However, the way the drug laws are currently established make it difficult for these companies to make a profit without charging a premium for new medicines. Every prescription drug on the market must go through the Food and Drug Administration (FDA), which takes several years of testing and retesting before approval can be granted. This is an expensive ordeal that has no guarantee of success, and any mistake post-approval opens the floodgate for legal retribution. Federal grants and funds ease the pain, but these companies are for-profit enterprises whose investors expect the company to earn significant returns, leaving them no choice but to pass the costs on to the consumer.

In addition, patent laws only protect these drugs for 20 years after the application is first filed. It takes the FDA an average of 7.5 years to approve a drug after the filing, which leaves only about a decade of exclusivity.[10]

Once the patent expires, other companies can essentially copy the previously protected drug and sell a cheaper alternative on the market. These "generic" medicines may have minute variations, and for some ailments these differences force patients to rely on the more expensive "trademark" brands.

Despite the challenges these companies face, the pharmaceutical industry is one of the largest players in the health care sector. These companies pull in between 300-400 billion dollars annually, with most of the money earned by selling brand-name drugs.[11] Though the timeframe to make substantial profits is small, pharmaceuticals still yield a large return by taking advantage of being the only available recourse for certain diseases.

Drugs are but one player in the substantial rise in health care costs. The market for drugs is never stagnant, as more medications are being released to deal with a variety of symptoms and diseases. While this rapid innovation is good for patients in terms of allowing individuals to live longer, the cost of these developments are spiking at the same pace.[12] Ultimately, in order to ensure that the drugs on the market are affordable, there needs to be a systematic change to the way medicine is sold, regulated, and advertised. We'll cover the potential solutions later in this chapter.

Taking Care of the Caretakers

We have covered some of the major players behind the health care market, but have yet to discuss the individuals and institutions responsible for actually caring for patients. Doctors, nurses, hospitals, and other medical centers face the impossible task of providing health care to millions of patients while participating in a system that has become increasingly dysfunctional. A career in medicine, once a position with stable and decent pay, is slowly growing out of favor, an alarming trend that signifies a shortage of necessary personnel.[13] Examining what medical professionals and facilities face on a regular basis will help us understand why changing the health care system is so challenging.

Hospitals are the most recognized symbol of modern health care. Over time, they have expanded to cover a wide range of services, and are where most individuals undergo major procedures such as surgery. Hospitals are also where almost all medical emergencies are processed, with a 24-hour emergency room (ER) staffed with doctors, nurses, and a variety of necessary equipment to keep patients alive. While there are always concerns regarding infections and inadequate resources, these institutions continue to serve as the first line of defense against serious ailments.

Thus, it is not surprising to assume that hospitals play a significant role in the rising cost of health care. As the *de facto* treatment center, many poor or sick patients rely on these facilities for medical services, knowing that the law prohibits these institutions from turning them away.[14] If these individuals cannot pay for care at the emergency center, the hospital has no choice but to absorb the losses through charging higher costs for more expensive procedures. This problem is compounded in rural areas, where the hospital may be the only major medical center in the region.

There may also be a strong profit motive for these institutions.[15] Hospitals, particularly those run by for-profit companies, expect to produce sufficient revenues on a regular basis. It is uncertain how much the rising cost can be attributed to the profit motive, and it should not be assumed that the status of a hospital impacts its prices more than other factors.

A recent development intended to serve as the cheaper alternative to hospitals is the rise of urgent care centers. Also known as "walk-in" clinics, they provide basic medical care at a lower rate than hospitals normally charge.[16] These institutions are not equipped to handle major or complex ailments, but they compensate by providing cheaper primary care and offer some preventative and emergency services. Walk-in clinics have seen significant growth in profits, and they are expected to continue growing over the next few decades.[17]

Urgent care centers are intended to provide an affordable alternative to overburdened and expensive hospitals. However, their effect on reducing health care costs has been remarkably minimal.[18] Walk-in clinics have yet to successfully siphon patients with minor ailments from the emergency room. In addition, urgent care centers tend to be located in wealthier, suburban areas, rather than poorer, underserved neighborhoods where they are needed most.[19]

Doctors With Borders

Doctors remain one of the most trusted professions in the United States, partially due to their education and expertise regarding matters of life and death.[20] These skilled individuals are highly compensated, in part because of strong barriers of entry, making it a desirable option for students willing to undergo rigorous training. However, the pressure on physicians is growing as the number of patients rise, with no promise or indication of increased compensation.

A trend that is alarming health care experts is the growing shortage of primary care doctors. Primary care or "family" physicians, who are the first to treat most ailments, are expected to be in high demand due to increased coverage under the Affordable Care Act.[21] However, in the United States, over two-thirds of all physicians are considered specialists, who perform specific procedures or focus on a particular organ system.[22]

This decline can be explained by two prime factors. First, the higher average pay for specialized practitioners stunts the incentive for medical students to become primary care physicians. Many medical students are seeking careers that will ensure the best return from their education, and the average compensation for family medicine is significantly lower than specialists.[23] The second problem is that the workload of general medical practitioners is rising faster than the number of available doctors.[24] The high demand of primary care along with the shortage of practicing physicians could create a frightening scenario of delayed care and wait-lists to see a medical professional.

Though doctors play a vital role in maintaining our health, nurses are one of the most underappreciated players within the health care sector. A doctor's time is best spent examining the medical information of a patient and deciding the best course of action, while nurses usually perform most of the other necessary tasks. The nursing staff and other ancillary personnel handle basic diagnostic tests, data collection, and other procedures.

There are several legal obstacles that hamper the potential efficiency of the nursing sector. Many nurses are required to work long hours, and are typically paid lower wages than their training should qualify them for. As a result, there is a growing shortage of registered nurses, sparking fears that there is not enough labor to care for new patients.[25]

Tort Reform at a Tortoise's Pace

One of the greatest headaches for doctors, hospitals, and medical facilities is the current malpractice landscape. Filing malpractice cases are rewarding for trial lawyers, who heavily advertise to lure lower-income individuals to file suit. In order to minimize the degree to which their personal assets are at risk in a dispute, doctors (and the facilities where the doctors work) purchase medical malpractice insurance at a high premium.[26] The purpose of this safety net is to provide medical staff an adequate defense in the event of a legal dispute. Malpractice insurance costs doctors tens of thousands of dollars or more annually, with greater costs depending on the risk of injury or misdiagnosis involved in that field.[27]

The money involved in malpractice suits and insurance premiums is not the only significant impact on the cost of medical care. Because of a deep-seated fear that failing to provide adequate care will lead to legal action, many doctors compensate by automatically taking redundant measures such as ordering extraneous tests. These practices are a significant resource drain for health care providers, and are mainly ordered to protect institutions and doctors from potential lawsuits.

When someone advocates for "tort reform," they generally seek to curb the worst abuses to the system by capping the rewards for a particular claim. More conservative states have enacted several measures aimed at reducing the pressure that potential lawsuits have on doctors.* Lawmakers must be careful to cap the compensation of damages to reasonable levels, but still allow patients or family members who suffered a clear case of negligence to receive adequate compensation to help resume their normal lives.[28]

The (Slightly More) Affordable Care Act

Although I support a majority of President Obama's policies, I have been ambivalent about the Patient Protection and Affordable Care Act (PPACA, or ACA for short) since it first passed Congress in 2010. I believe that the initiative was a step in the right direction by preventing some of the worst practices by insurance companies and hospitals, such as denying care for "pre-existing conditions." In addition, the law expanded coverage for young people under their parent's plan until 26 years of age.

However, to say that this law is the ultimate panacea for our health care woes is an unsubstantiated claim. There are several aspects of the health care sector that the law does not address, particularly high costs for employers and tort reform. There is also the question of cost to the government, which will likely increase as programs such as Medicare and Medicaid consume more tax revenues.

Still, it is worth understanding the significance of passing such legislation. By enacting this bill, Obama has solidified the government's role in shaping the health care market. The medical industry was long overdue for a shake-up, and the development of this law encouraged a necessary national conversation regarding the chronic issues facing this sector.

Opponents of the law have offered no alternative, only their populist resentment. Thus far, the "anti-Obamacare" crowd has failed to provide a reputable and logical course for the future of health care.[29] Unfortunately, Democratic policymakers are wary of proposing any necessary changes, as it would allow conservatives to claim how the ACA was a complete failure. Republicans, on the other hand, have no significant alternative to address the problems facing the health care system, and are fearful that admitting the benefits would infuriate their supporters. Regardless of who wins the White House in 2016, it is unlikely that the next administration will repeal the law.

The most controversial aspect of this law is the insurance mandate, which requires every US citizen to have or acquire health care coverage, or pay a penalty. While this seems to be an intrusive government mandate, it is actually based on economic principles.[30] Theoretically, a health insurance "pool" should include a wide variety of people in their plans. However, prior to the ACA many healthy individuals chose not to sign up for coverage, and a significant portion of the insured were chronically ill individuals. This led to many insurance companies exploiting loopholes to deny care for sick people.

An insurance mandate would solve two simultaneous problems. First, forcing healthy people to have insurance places a reduced burden on insurance companies to provide care. By having a more consistent stream of income, these companies would be able to cover care for patients with chronic diseases. The other improvement that the insurance mandate provides is that when healthy individuals become sick or receive a traumatic injury, they have a safety net in place to cover most of the costs. This ensures that more fit individuals are not burdening the system because they only seek benefits when they are ill.

When the Supreme Court ruled 5-4 in *National Federation of Independent Businesses vs. Sebelius* (2012) that the insurance mandate, along with most of the ACA, was constitutional, an intense shock rippled throughout the political landscape.[31] Chief Justice John Roberts, a relatively conservative judge who favors restraining the federal government's powers, sided with the more progressive justices to uphold almost the entire law. The reason for Robert's vote is uncertain, but Justice Ruth Ginsburg's concurrence points out the necessity of the insurance mandate for the health care system to function. The government, she argues, needs this power because all individuals at some point will need medical care, regardless of their current health. Subsequently, it is in the best interest of the country to ensure proper care.

One of the changes that occurred under the ACA is the creation of the state-based insurance marketplace. The federal government, along with participating state governments, host a catalog of private health coverage for individuals to browse and select. Originally, every state would be required to partake in creating a marketplace, but the Supreme Court ruled that action an unconstitutional violation of federalism. Therefore, citizens in non-participating states must rely on the federal exchange.

By insuring previously uninsured individuals, the domestic economy is likely to benefit in the long run.[32] Enrolling all citizens in this new plan will provide a steadier stream of income for insurance providers, reducing the incentive to cut benefits. In addition, being forced to cover chronically ill patients who were previously denied coverage would reduce the expense these individuals will face in the future, potentially improving their productive capacity.

Predictions in a static medium such as this book are risky, especially those dealing with recent political events. However, I believe that the marketplace will either be a spectacular success or a transitional method towards covering the American citizenry with insurance. I almost guarantee that the Affordable Care Act will not be the only change to health care, as an evolving medical industry will adapt to (or exploit) these new circumstances over time.

Government Good, Business Bad

The alternatives suggested by those who favor expanding government insurance should be briefly addressed. The United States is one of the few developed countries where the government does not cover its citizen's health insurance. Since these countries also have lower overall health care costs than the US, many progressives assume that the profit motives behind for-profit medical companies are the primary cause of higher costs. As a result, they conclude, only the government should provide health care coverage, which eliminates the constant drive for more revenue.

Implementing a "single-payer" system, in which the government is the only party responsible for providing insurance, would solve the problem of people not being able to access care. However, outside of the (expensive) bureaucratic nightmare that will arise from eliminating private insurance, government-run health care cannot address all of the factors leading to higher costs. The number of patients a doctor treats is already growing, and having the government immediately insure everyone would lead to diminished care. This could also contribute to the formal implementation of wait-lists, the largest criticism by conservatives of government-run health care.[33]

The alternative to single-payer would be to create a "public option" for insurance. This would essentially allow individuals to sign up for an insurance plan run by the federal government, with no strings attached. This option does not disqualify other private companies from providing insurance, but it does force them to compete with the government to provide affordable health care. However, as with single-payer, it does not address some of the core causes of medical inflation.

If implementing a single-payer or public option program attempts to lower costs by significantly reducing reimbursements for doctors and other essential medical staff, we may see an unintended labor shortage in this sector.[34] Such a crisis cannot be easily corrected, as the market forces that normally influence a doctor's pay are not powerful enough under a single-payer or public option system. Thus, the government would have to either artificially increase medical wages through tax benefits (which raises the average tax bill), or reduce the services medical facilities can provide. Neither of these options is preferable, and indicates how complex factors cause overly simplistic solutions to fail. I do not think that government-run health insurance is a flawed concept in and of itself, but we must account for all factors influencing the rising cost of medicine before entrusting our health care system to the public sector.

An Apple a Day

The good news is that the internal market forces, and potentially the expected effects of the Affordable Care Act, has lead to a slowdown of rising medical costs for consumers.[35] While this is welcome news for all parties, it is too early to say that we are done reforming health care. At this point, let us discuss further changes that are necessary to ensure the affordability and quality of health care in the United States. Many of these suggestions would be difficult to implement due to social, legal, economic, or political obstacles. However, if policymakers and the public are serious about wanting a more stable medical sector, it is important to consider the options below.

It is nearly impossible, even in the age of the Internet, to ascertain the overall cost of certain medical procedures. Part of the problem is that there is no central list or commonly used site that publishes or offers this information. In addition, Medicare/Medicaid reimbursement rates for procedures are insufficient to gauge an overall price range. Surprisingly, most doctors are unaware of the true cost of the procedures they perform.[36] Without price transparency, the health care market is incapable of effective competition, which explains why prices can vary substantially within the same area.

However, in 2013 the Department of Health and Human Services (HHS) released a spreadsheet of the average price and amount paid for the most common procedures at every major medical institution.[37] HHS released this information under the assumption that price transparency would lead to lower overall costs, as hospitals will now be able to compete with one another. Unfortunately, most consumers and institutions are unaware of this publication, dampening the potential shockwaves to the market. It is my hope that the regular release of this information will, over time, lead to less fluctuations in cost, and encourage hospitals to control the outlandish prices of some of their procedures.

Of course, price transparency means nothing during medical emergencies. Patients cannot make a rational purchasing decision when their health is in danger, and often have no choice as to where they end up receiving care.[38] Thus, the burden to reduce the cost of emergency procedures rests with hospitals and the government. One way to achieve this is to reduce ER visits by giving medical centers the option to automatically divert non-emergency cases to urgent care centers or other institutions, where the cost of care is likely to be cheaper.

Privatization is often seen as a force for good, by encouraging lower costs and improved efficiency. However, in the case of for-profit ambulance companies, the benefits of competition have not been seen. To my knowledge, there have been several cases where a family member or friend was transported by a private ambulance and was charged three times as much as one that is publicly owned. If privatization does nothing to reduce the price of a public service, than there is no purpose to allowing this trend to continue.[39]

I mentioned earlier that Justice Ruth Ginsburg's concurring opinion notes that it is impossible for someone to remain isolated from the health care market. It is safe to imply that the behaviors and practices of our fellow citizens, the institutions they receive care from, and the types of procedures they need will directly impact everyone else's medical bills. Thus, it is in the best interest of the United States to encourage the majority of its citizens to live healthy, active lives.

The United States currently has the second highest rates of overweight citizens (Mexico took the reigns as the fattest nation recently). Obesity is a huge resource drain on the population, causing people to be at a greater risk for a buffet of health issues.[40] The cause of our bulging bellies is somewhat complex, but can be boiled down to an overabundance of sugar and carbohydrates in our diet combined with a lack of proper exercise. This phenomenon of high obesity (personally, I prefer the term "fat-nomenon") leads to many errors in proper diagnosis, and can impact the effectiveness of certain procedures.

The government, insurance companies, and employers should encourage individuals to modify their behaviors. For instance, businesses can offer financial incentives for establishing a regular exercise routine, or offer healthy food options at sponsored events. In addition, First Lady Michelle Obama is attempting to discourage childhood obesity through her "Let's Move" campaign, which tackles weight issues before they are established in adulthood. However, it is important to ensure that measures to reduce obesity take into account the circumstances of each individual. For instance, enacting a tax on highly fattening foods could lead to less consumption, but may unfairly punish poorer individuals who cannot afford healthier options.

Along with obesity, other risky behaviors such as smoking and binge drinking should be suppressed (but not banned) to reduce the burden these activities place on health care. Personal liberty is important for democratic nations such as ours to function, but when they endanger society there needs to be some limits to behaviors that greatly impact our health. Is society willing to give up indulgences and temporary pleasures to ensure the stability of our medical system? If our nation were to lead a healthier lifestyle, medical care would become more affordable.

The issue of tort reform is a partisan battlefield, with progressives favoring the rights of those who were wronged by medical "mistakes," while conservatives defend the doctors facing unnecessary and frivolous accusations. While I lean moderate-left on most issues, I must defect from my fellow progressives and stand in favor of critically examining the current malpractice landscape. The costs of potential and actual lawsuits are far too great for health care providers, and there are not enough protections for doctors and institutions providing care. While individuals should have the capacity to sue those who have wronged them or their family, there needs to be limits on the potential compensation victims can receive. Tort laws vary by state, so the movement to change these laws must start on the local level.

Reducing the potential shortage of primary care doctors should be a clear priority for governments and medical institutions. One of the most common (and perhaps the most effective) suggestions to address this problem is to reduce the cost of medical school through grants and tax incentives for future family physicians. Already, the Obama Administration has pledged to significantly invest in training these types of practitioners, and institutions are increasing the residency slots devoted to primary care.[41] Another option is to provide primary care education for free or at a reduced rate for top-ranking students, but require them to serve in poorer communities for a specific number of years. The military has already implemented similar training programs, and this concept could be expanded to civilian doctors.

As I stated earlier in this chapter, the greatest change to the health care sector is the integration of new technologies in medicine. Innovations in this field will come naturally as the market advances, but there needs to be a major push to improve efficiency in the way practitioners handle a patient's information. Currently, there is little communication between health institutions when it comes to providing a patient's medical history, forcing doctors to order redundant tests.[42] In addition, many doctors and other medical staff are not adequately trained to use electronic health records that store a patient's information.

Adopting technology will reduce time spent documenting medical information, and saves the health care system from being overrun with newly covered patients. Already, paper is being replaced with tablets and laptops, and easily transferable medical files will reduce the likelihood of other doctors from ordering unnecessary procedures or tests.[43] Improved preventative technology will likely be able to identify symptoms of a disease sooner, which can save patients and doctors time and money. However, none of these developments can occur at a rapid rate without standardization.

I propose the creation of a universal patient information document, an equivalent of a ".doc" for medicine, that can be transferred from one party to another. The best means of formulating this standard can only arise from a global consortium of medical institutions, technology companies, and the government. There are rudimentary formats already in place, such as HL7 (a basic patient information schema) and DICOM (which allows the transfer of medical images, such as X-rays), but none are comprehensive or interoperable.[44]

For the successful implementation of this concept, only licensed medical facilities should be able to obtain the software necessary to use this information, which would prevent outside hackers from easily abusing sensitive data. Having a standard throughout the medical field would enable patients to easily transfer their prior records (which may or may not be digital) when they change doctors or need a specific procedure. While there will always be privacy risks regarding this information, encryption and security clearance should be sufficient enough to prevent widespread abuse. Eventually, the cost savings this plan provides would quickly make up for the initial investment.

The changes we will see in health care is similar to an aircraft carrier changing course. New regulations and technology will take time to be fully implemented, and it may occasionally seem as if the ship is not moving. However, the ship is slowly turning, and will eventually steer toward a sustainable path. It will be interesting to see what developments will occur in health care during the 21st century, as it will determine the overall direction of the marketplace as a whole.

*One of the prime funding sources for the Democratic Party are trial lawyers, so it makes sense as to why progressive politicians are hesitant to enact such policies. It also explains why Republicans are so eager to enact tort reform, outside of the reasons stated in this section.

Chapter 8

Money, Currencies, and the Dollar

Federal Reserve Building in Washington, DC, July 11, 2012

A WALLET IS AN INTRIGUING REFLECTION of an individual. These pocket-sized packs contain many items necessary for daily life, such as identification, cash, credit cards, and perhaps pictures of one's family. Losing a wallet often feels like a terrifying experience, as someone could easily use the contents for malicious deeds. Thanks to modern developments, however, most of these items are easy to replace (except the cash, of course) or nullify. Banks can cancel stolen credit cards in just a few minutes, and replacement IDs are now relatively easy to obtain. Still, a wallet is the key that drives the economic engine, and represents the consumer culture we have grown to accept.

In my wallet, I regularly carry a certain amount of cash, my debit and credit cards, various membership cards, and other objects of interest. These items are vital for my daily routine, yet the most prized possession I carry in my pocket is a 500-yen (¥) coin. Although I carry paper currency worth more than the Japanese mint (¥500 is currently worth around $5), it still holds great value to me, as it reminds me of my first trip abroad. This is a common example of the difference between the perceived value of an item versus the actual value, a lesson that is central to economics and the concept of money.

This section covers how we perceive currency, and how the US dollar plays a significant role in the global economy. I will examine the potential threats that could undermine its value (literally and metaphorically), and address suggested alternatives pondered by intellectuals. In addition, with the rise of crypto-currencies such as Bitcoin, I also hope to share my predictions regarding the future of money. Monetary policy is a confusing realm for most people, so the use of jargon and technical language will be kept to a minimum.

Many people mistake economics as "the study of money."[1] Although currency is the primary focus of most economists, it is only one aspect of the field. Experts follow currency exchange rates, alterations to the money supply, and actions taken by major financial institutions, such as the Federal Reserve, as a means to evaluate the health of the global economy.*

In most other chapters, I present a characteristic of capitalism that needs improvement, and provide solutions or suggestions that could resolve our economic problems in the long term. However, the monetary policy of the United States presently has no significant hurdles that threaten its welfare. Instead, I want to devote this section to evaluating the state of the US dollar and discuss potential changes to the money market, along with the costs and benefits of those alterations.

Follow the Rules, Follow the Money

Money in and of itself has three primary purposes.[2] First, it is the standard for which all goods and services are valued in a participating economy. In other words, we use money to evaluate how much a particular item costs, within the limits of supply and demand. Currency-based markets work better than a barter system, where it is difficult for merchants and property owners to evaluate the fairness of a trade.

The second reason we use money is because it serves as storage of value. How can you be certain that the money in your bank or the coins stuck in your couch cushions are worth something? Society has unofficially agreed through a "social contract" that this currency has a certain value that does not quickly decay. Holding this asset represents an obligation that is owed to you, be it in the form of products or services.

The third and most visible purpose of money is as a medium of exchange. Trading money for goods and services represents a transfer of value from one person to another. When economists track the Gross Domestic Product (GDP), they rely upon the value of all economic transactions that take place in a country.[3] Thus, if GDP falls compared to the prior year, it is because the amount of money exchanged has lessened, signaling a reduction in overall spending and income.

In addition to the functions of money, it is essential to note why we use coins or paper as currency in the first place. Most stable currencies are crafted in such a way to hold little physical or commercial value, and are only backed through social and legal recognition.[4] Coins are made using a precise mixture of materials, and when melted down yield only a speck of precious metals. Paper currencies are usually favored for higher-valued legal tender, as the materials needed to make it are cheap and plentiful.

There are other purposes and advantages to using money, but the principles mentioned above are essential for agencies that determine a nation's monetary policy. It is remarkably easy for a currency to suddenly raise its value exponentially, and then crash once a market disruption occurs. The financial horror stories you hear about runaway inflation and currencies used as "wallpaper" stem from a failure to uphold any or all of the qualifications for sound money.[5]

Hello Dollar

Most citizens of the United States take the US dollar (USD) for granted. However, they do not understand how widely accepted it is around the world. Scholars disagree on the precise numbers, but between 30-40 percent of all US dollars in circulation ends up overseas.[6] This unofficially makes the USD the most widely used non-native currency on the planet, with the Euro in a strong second-place position.[7]

The US dollar is considered by the global market to be the most stable legal tender, and is the largest reserve currency for the majority of the world. Most international transactions take place in USD, and almost all central banks outside the United States hold a significant amount of dollars in their reserve.[8] The dollar is distributed by the US Treasury and managed by the Federal Reserve, which must balance the two conflicting goals of reducing unemployment and controlling inflation.[9] Because the modern Fed avoids many common policy pitfalls, many businesses and individuals feel comfortable maintaining their assets in this form.

Why, of all the other currencies, does the US dollar earn the distinction of the world's default method of exchange? The main reason rests on several factors, the most prominent being the sheer size of the United States economy.[10] If international firms seek to enter US markets or receive investment from American firms, they tend to rely on using the dollar for most large transactions. It also helps that most sales using other currencies are measured against the USD, as stability allows a proper measurement of the "true" value of a trade.

However, market size alone does not solidify one's standing to be the most widely used method of exchange. Government and economic stability are crucial to maintaining the trust of businesses worldwide.[11] The United States government, while not perfect, is unlikely to experience political or military revolutions. In addition to being politically secure, the United States has little risk of experiencing a rapid financial collapse. Though we came close in 2008, when toxic assets nearly froze the money market, the government stepped in (with varying results) to ensure that banks remain open to loan capital to domestic and international businesses. Thus, it is reasonable to assume that the dollar will remain guaranteed by the US for many decades to come.

The desire for consistency is also why the Chinese Yuan (or Renmimbi, if you're a stickler for technicality), despite being used in the second-largest economy, has not gained prominence as an international currency. The rapid growth China is experiencing is currently favorable for outside investors, but their currency faces a substantial risk of instability.[12] Corruption and the lack of a democratic process partially erode long-term faith in the capacity of Chinese leaders to control the value of the Yuan.

Popular Paranoia

Despite the international good standing of the dollar, there are individuals and groups who believe that the current money market is disadvantageous to its citizens. Their prime concern stems from the fact that there is nothing technically backing the dollar, and expansionary policies may fuel inflation to unsustainable levels.[13] In addition, certain individuals fear that at some point the United States will be unable to honor its debts, and the dollar will essentially become useless.

These fears held by Fed opponents originate from two assumptions, both of which yield a populist tone. The first is that the Federal Reserve is technically quasi-private, and naturally seeks the best interest for the institution itself.[14] There is little accountability in determining what actions the Fed is capable of taking, and Congress has done little to stop them. In addition, individuals who have strong ties to the banking world set our monetary policy.[15]

The other common complaint is the vast amount of discretion the government gives to the Fed. There is a vocal minority that opposes the Federal Reserve, and seeks to limit its power or authorities. Certain members of Congress have proposed legislation that would force the Fed to reduce its flexibility to alter the money supply and provide "transparency" in ways that would limit its ability to impact the markets.[16]

While efforts to further decentralize the regulation of the money supply is philosophically pleasing, they carry a huge risk of destabilizing the dollar. Eliminating or severely limiting the Federal Reserve would reduce the capacity for effective expansionary monetary policy during recessions.[17] In addition, many individuals who oppose the Federal Reserve either have significant investments in proposed alternatives, such as commodity-backed currencies, or seek to undermine government power in general.[18] They also underestimate the use of the dollar in international markets and ignore how changes to the currency could threaten its "super-currency" status.

As you have probably guessed, I am not convinced by the arguments of opponents of the Federal Reserve. It is important to remember that although the institution is technically private, it is established and supported by the federal government and serves as the nation's central bank. The reason the Fed was created in 1913 was to have an institution of experts immune to political pressures setting monetary policy.[19] The leadership (known as the Board of Governors) is composed mostly of bankers and economists, who are nominated by the President and approved by Congress. Although it has made historic mistakes, time has only empowered the Federal Reserve as an economic force. The Fed is staffed with highly intelligent experts on money management. These individuals are essentially civil servants based on merit, and have salaries predetermined by law.

Golden Age of Gold-Less Money

Even though I have established that the concerns regarding the legitimacy of our monetary system are largely unfounded, it would be imprudent to ignore any potential suggestions to change our current structure. Many proposals have been laid out as an alternative to what critics see as an unsustainable system.[20] To address potential issues to our currency, monetary policy experts should examine and critique proposed alternatives.

The prime alternative often cited as a better means of storing value is attaching our money to a valuable commodity. Metals such as gold, silver and platinum have been used as money for several millennia, relying upon their rarity and durability to ensure high value.[21] Bank notes backed by these commodities are cited as the most common preference over the current system, though other highly desired resources have been suggested.

The use of "floating currencies," or money that is not backed by anything of material value, is a relatively recent phenomenon. The United States has historically switched back and forth between tying its currency to gold and leaving it as a fiat note.[22] The US dollar has remained gold-free since 1971, when President Richard Nixon, in an attempt to prevent widespread inflation, removed all ties to gold and let the dollar's value be determined by the markets.

Commodity backed money is mainly appealing to libertarians, as it prevents the government from arbitrarily determining the value of currencies. Having the dollar tied to commodities (such as gold) follows free market principles, and ensures that the medium of exchange is actually backed by something of value.[23] In addition, because the supply of gold is set, the threat of inflation is significantly lower, as the money supply is fixed based on the amount of gold available on the market.

However, all of these assumptions immediately fail the moment an economic downturn occurs.[24] The government is unable to increase the money supply to stimulate the economy, as the amount of gold on the market is limited and alchemy is confined to the realm of fiction. In addition, guaranteeing bank notes with a certain amount of gold runs the risk of widespread gold hoarding. With more people holding on to their savings, a drop in spending is inevitable, which leads to lower revenues and investment capital. Commodity backers may claim that the market can "self-correct," but the Great Depression proved that correction is not always quick or easy.

Commodity based currencies are also difficult to justify in the modern world due to the rapid growth in human population. It may have been possible to guarantee an exchange of bank notes for gold or other materials in the past, but there are simply not enough of these materials to provide every person on the planet with their fair share. In addition, the glut for new resources could instigate greater environmental degradation, which ultimately impairs economic growth and productivity in the long run.[25]

There is not a single nation attached to the gold standard in modern times, and there is no apparent rush to do so. Inflation for most developed countries has remained relatively low, an indication of an adequate and flexible money supply. Monetary policy experts also recognize how difficult it is to implement commodity-backed currencies in our modern economy. Because globalization is centered on fiat-based transactions, and only a select few countries have the majority of certain commodities, it would be impossible to ensure a fair economic playing field.

Fictional Fight with the Fed

The other major alternative to our current system is to decentralize monetary authority away from the Federal Reserve. This argument follows the libertarian doctrine of a limited, decentralized government, and allows monetary policy to be set by several other institutions, akin to democratic principles.[26] This would expand the role of local and state banks to act appropriately to local economic changes, while limiting the Federal Reserve to maintain a prescribed money supply and remain the lending bank of last resort.

Such a proposal may have seemed reasonable a few decades ago, but the prime issue with decentralization is that the economy is becoming increasingly interconnected. Local economies are not isolated, and are heavily influenced by the well-being of the national and international economy.[27] The proposals given by decentralization advocates completely ignore the role of the Federal Reserve to promote economic activity. There is also no guarantee that the interests and goals of local banks are synced with the needs of the national markets.

There are other changes that have been suggested, but none have shown promise as a viable solution. In the end, most people do not care how their money is backed or who gives it to them, as long as there is a semblance of stability. One of the greatest success stories of the post-2008 recovery is that, while income took a significant hit, we managed to avoid deflation.[28] In other words, the purchasing power of the dollar held by the public retained the same overall value. This is crucial to understand as we consider how we use our money in the 21st century.

Magic Internet Money

Technically, cash and checks are only two forms of "currency" that are considered part of the primary money supply. However, the rise of credit and debit cards has transformed the way we comprehend finance. Almost every legitimate business accepts these forms of payment, and is encouraging international trade through online venues such as Amazon.

The prime concern regarding credit cards is that they lead to widespread indebtedness.[29] While credit card debt remains a serious problem, it has also accelerated the economy by providing a faster and more convenient method of exchange for responsible businesses. Debit cards, though more restricted in use, allow individuals to easily and quickly access their funds via ATMs.

With the ability to easily purchase goods comes a greater risk of fraud, and stealing credit card numbers and information online has never been easier for opportunistic hackers.[30] There has been a spike in digital attacks aimed at obtaining information from private companies. With financial information being increasingly stored online, it has become easier for malicious individuals or terrorist groups to obtain access to our most critical financial institutions.[31]

As our financial information is increasingly being stored on vulnerable servers, a counter-movement has emerged with the goal of allowing private transactions to take place over the Internet. In the midst of writing this book, a new financial phenomenon arose in the form of Bitcoin. Created by Satoshi Nakamoto (whose real identity is still unknown at the time of print), and backed by libertarian-minded and technologically savvy individuals, this "crypto-currency" is attempting to turn the tide against the practice of tracking purchases.

Bitcoin and other digital currencies work through complex means, but the idea is that the transfer of payment is far cheaper and faster than more conventional means, such as credit card and bank transfer fees.[32] In addition, there is no central bank or country that regulates Bitcoin, thus anyone in any country can theoretically accept it. Because crypto-currencies are usually tied to an account based on a local computer's hard drive, it is difficult for hackers to obtain access to someone's account.[33] Of course, the biggest caveat to this security is that accidentally losing your hard drive prior to a manual transfer means that you also lose access to your account. For privacy advocates and libertarian economists, Bitcoin is one of the best innovations in free market capitalism in recent memory.

However, I warn against the common person to become heavily invested in services like Bitcoin, at least for the moment. Because there is an extensive amount of interest in crypto-currencies, many are experiencing rapid changes in value, making it an unstable and risky storage of value.** In addition, there is no limitation to the capacity of fraud, as transfers cannot be reversed.[34] The greatest benefactor to this new service is likely to be the black market, which can easily hide their transactions from governments.

The international response to Bitcoin and other Internet currencies has been mixed at best. Certain nations or trading blocs are unwilling to promote the currency due to a lack of consumer protections and control, while others have banned it outright.[35] Interestingly enough, the United States government, which is openly at odds with illicit trade, is the country that has most openly welcomed the currency as a promising concept. Our policymakers' greatest concern stems mainly from the difficulty of taxing transactions over these services, which could reduce revenues for essential government programs.[36]

Bitcoin is unlikely to remain a viable currency, but it serves as an interesting experiment to determine the safest means of storing and transferring funds online. Although formal trade systems have thrived since the beginning of civilization, the online economy is effectively younger than the author of this book. Given that so much has changed in just two decades, it is exciting to consider the prospects of payment and transactions in the future.

"Please Send 1 Million USD"

Presently, the US dollar is not facing any particular threats to its stability and value. It is currently safe from minor economic calamities, and is the continuing "reserve currency" for countries where the native legal tender has fallen apart.[37] As a whole, the Federal Reserve and Congress have done a satisfactory job maintaining faith in the US dollar. However, there are financial and political forces that could open a Pandora's box of financial woes if not appropriately accounted for.

The Euro-zone countries are currently in a state of monetary limbo. The debt crisis, involving Greece, Italy, Spain and potentially other EU countries, has been a chronic fear for European investors over the past few years.[38] While it seems that the worst is behind us, there is no guarantee that countries participating in the European Union will retain their current policies if opposing political parties win elections.

Suppose the worst-case scenario occurs, and the Euro suffers considerably or crashes outright. One would assume this would be beneficial for the US, as it would increase the demand for the dollar, boosting its purchasing power. However, the combination of a shock in the money market and a recession throughout Europe would lead to a similar economic downturn in the United States.[39] While a stronger dollar could make foreign goods more affordable, we would quickly see income drop as exports take a dive. Such a scenario is becoming increasingly unlikely, but financial institutions should continue observing the value of their European assets.

Europe is not the only region that should concern international markets. Since the economy has become increasingly globalized, instability in any nation with a large supply of essential resources is guaranteed to shake the US dollar's value. We learned from the 1970s that a sudden supply shock is capable of catastrophic economic damage.[40] If the equivalent of the 1973 oil embargo occurred today, the US dollar would spiral out of control, requiring drastic action from central banks and governments around the world. Globalization, though a powerful force for economic good, can either diminish or exacerbate the impact of rapid supply shifts. A resource shock in countries with a smaller pool of resources is unlikely to inflict major harm to the US, but incidents in nations that have a near monopoly on these goods could easily trigger a worldwide recession.

Daft Punk Dollar

The Federal Reserve celebrated its 100th anniversary in December 2013. In the century of its existence, the Fed has experienced many challenges. The worst economic downturn in recorded history, the rise of the US dollar as a global currency, a complete reexamination of classical economic literature, hyperinflation, returning to and dropping the gold standard, and several minor and major recessions have all tested the resilience of our monetary system. It would be foolish to state that monetary policy can now settle into a familiar pattern, as rapid technological changes prove that the future is difficult to predict.

It is safe to assume that the US Dollar, at least for the first half of the 21st century, will remain the dominant (or one of the dominant) global currencies. Though there is considerable pressure from far-right and far-left ideologues to modify the practices of the Federal Reserve, there is little incentive for policymakers and economists to enact major changes. Thus, we can expect the Fed to continue to be a powerful force in the world of finance.

However, this influence will be harder to maintain, as international affairs and politics increasingly alter the direction of the US economy. We import and export more goods and services than any other country, and invest a greater amount of capital overseas.[41] Thus, it is easy to assume that the economic well being of other countries will determine the demand for the dollar. United States policymakers should continue the momentum of foreign economic activity inside and outside our borders, and foresee how any shift in purchases abroad could impact the demand for US currency.

As more transactions take place online, the use of physical currency is likely to decline over time. Technical innovations such as Google Wallet and PayPal reduce the need to carry large amounts of cash. However, I am not ready to declare the death of coins and paper prematurely. A significant number of businesses rely on physical currency to earn income, and cash is still a convenient method of exchange. There are also privacy concerns, as companies that store financial data are common targets for hackers.

Bitcoin will either stabilize or be destroyed, but crypto-currencies still hold promise in the 21st century. Given the diminished personal privacy that has emerged along with modern technology, people want a means, outside of cash, to pay for goods and services without a clear method of tracking. Although crypto-currencies are likely to be used for criminal purposes, governments should not block this innovation and force all transactions to be traceable.

One final prediction that is worth considering is the rise of other regional currencies. The (relative) success of the Euro could prompt other economically similar regions, such as Latin America or Africa, to enter trade blocs and print multi-national coins and paper notes. If successful, we may see the consolidation of smaller currencies into larger ones. Whether or not this occurs will depend on how the Euro will continue to weather its current economic calamities.

Capitalism does not require money to exist, but it is the foundation for a simple means of exchanging valuable goods. Thus, it is important to understand how our modern society perceives its money to implement effective monetary policy. The status quo that serves us now may not be the best strategy for managing our currency in the future, and we may need to reconsider our valuation of the dollar to respond to new trends.

The Federal Reserve and similar institutions serve as the anchor for the capitalist ship. Without this essential tool, our vessel may steer too far off course, and would drift away from its intended destination. It is my hope that the US dollar remains a stable and active lubricant to the economic engine, and that we are willing to take measures to protect the full faith and credit of the United States.

*The Federal Reserve, for those who are unaware, is the quasi-government agency responsible for managing the United States money supply, and for setting monetary policy for the country. Congress is technically entitled to this power, but considering the lackluster financial qualifications of the average Congress member, they wisely delegate the "Fed" to do the heavy lifting.

**Within a week of this chapter's inception, the value of one Bitcoin fluctuated by almost 200 US dollars.

Chapter 9

Debt

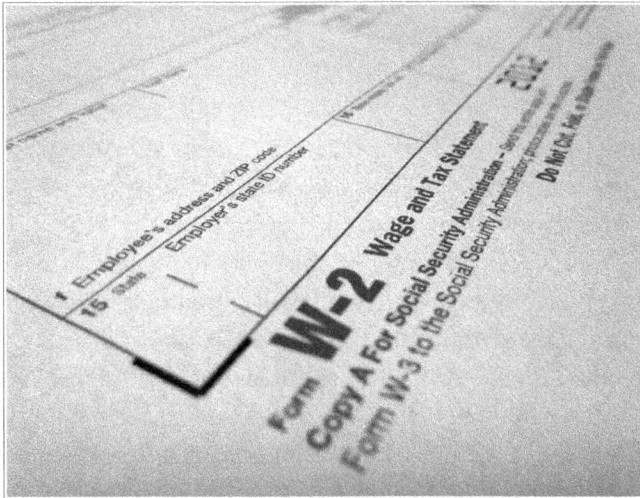

W-2 Wage and Tax Statement

WHEN MOST PEOPLE IMAGINE the word "debt," they think about people stuck with an endless sea of bills, or the government's incapacity to spend less than it receives. However, economists view it as one of the most important concepts in economics.[1] Debt is an essential tool of trade, as it reduces the burden of limited personal assets, which allows people to take greater risks. Using loans from outside sources, businesses are able to purchase tools or goods, and individuals can purchase higher valued assets such as a car or home.

However, debt can be a trap for bad decisions or poor judgment, and it is too easy to have one's credit self-destruct in a short time. Many people mistakenly take out large loans when their current income is not set in stone, which is extraordinarily risky for workers in sectors that have a high turnover rate. In addition, there are many unethical business schemes that lure individuals in with instant "rewards," only to later slap the poor consumers with incredibly high interest rates.[2]

This chapter focuses on the topic of debt, covering both the private and public sectors. Because the last financial crisis was centered on (and caused by) liabilities, it is important to understand how much our economy relies on debts to function. I will cover the most common debts (such as housing and education) and highlight the disturbing trends that surround greater obligations. In addition, as concerns regarding the fiscal situation of the federal government grow, we are likely to enter a period of significantly reduced expenditures (and possibly higher taxes).

I Owe You

The concept of debt has been around for thousands of years, emerging alongside the concept of money. Society relies upon the notion of lending to grow economically and has developed systems that enable people to give and receive loans. However, not all of these systems were fair or properly enforced, and entire generations of families were tied to a lifetime of obligation.[3]

In modern times, there are several rules that ensure fairness to the person or business procuring and providing the loan. Most countries have formal rules that require a contract between the party offering the loan (usually a bank) and the person or group that receives it. The borrower is indebted to pay back the loan and any additional interest. While this seems simple enough, there are many cases where one side fails their end of the bargain. This creates a difficult mess that most institutions seek to avoid.

To determine the likelihood of a successful loan, lenders often rely upon the credit history of the recipient. It used to be much harder to determine the creditworthiness of an individual or business, as communication between institutions was delayed depending on the distance between them. Today, there are specific institutions that provide financial information regarding the trustworthiness of a borrower. In the United States, major businesses are ranked by credit rating agencies such as Standard & Poor's, Moody's, and Fitch (also known as the Big Three).[4] Equifax, TransUnion, and Experian create a "credit score" that reflects the ability of individuals to pay obligations such as bills and loans. Having a low credit rating or credit score is one of the primary reasons banks refuse to give out loans.

However, the trust in these institutions, specifically the Big Three, has weakened since the financial system nearly collapsed in 2008. Because many of the subprime mortgage loans they initially ranked as AAA were actually highly unstable, many investors were misled into believing there was no risk in profiting from bad loans.[5] As a result, companies and governments have scrutinized these agencies, and have altered financial rules to prevent the same scenario from returning. More recently, the United States government's credit rating by Standard and Poor's dropped from AAA to AA+, but it had no impact on the purchasing rate of government bonds.[6]

Although credit rating agencies have faulted in the past decade, it is still important that such institutions remain in place. The difference between a AA and AA- rating may only be important to the most meticulous of investors. However, when businesses must choose between working with a AA- rated company or a B+ rated company, the safest choice is clearly the best. Credit rating companies have slowly regained the trust of businesses and governments, and it is unlikely that they will fall apart anytime soon.

Brother, Can You Spare 3% Interest

It is likely that you, dear reader, are in possession of some form of debt. The average American devotes about 10% of their total household income to paying off outstanding debts.[7] The convenience of household debt is that it gives individuals breathing room to pay for certain goods and services, as opposed to the conventional means of being charged up front. Many successful businesses started through funds borrowed from outside institutions such as banks.

However, the last economic crisis demonstrate how debt can be both a blessing and a curse, as the financial crisis lead to a significant decline in the capacity to pay off obligations. Millions of Americans were forced to endure high mortgage costs for a house that was worth less that the amount owed to the lending bank, a consequence of the housing crash. Foreclosures have fortunately fallen from their peak during the recession, but many families are barely able to pay off their loans to this day.[8]

In addition to the crippling debt caused by the recession, many individuals saw their credit scores suffer.[9] Some jobless homeowners were faced with the frightening decision of abandoning their mortgaged home, and incurring a substantial hit to their credit score. Others simply borrowed more money to pay for other bills, running deeper into debt. The federal government stepped in to prevent banks from aggressively pursuing these households, but there are still many families wading through the waters.[10]

Abandoning those who have suffered financially from the most recent economic downturn will have a damaging impact on the economy in the long run. Although debt can accelerate economic growth, too much of it can quickly reverse the short-term gains made, as most income would be dedicated to paying off loans.[11] As a result, it is in the best interest of homeowners, businesses, and governments to act quickly to protect those who still suffer from the ramifications of high mortgage payments.

The government (or, ideally, banking institutions) should improve the capacity for individuals to refinance their mortgages to better reflect their income prospects and current home value. As the housing market finally shows signs of growth, now is the best time to implement such programs. It is also in the best interest of banks to take a potential profit loss in return for the assurance that homeowners can pay off debts. These programs should also be isolated from credit score review, as the situation many homeowners experienced during the crash cannot be judged through a fair lens.

Another proposal to improve the prospects of homeowners is to mandate a permanent credit "bump" by the scoring agencies. This arbitrary inflation should not be more than 10% of one's current average credit, and should only apply to individuals who took out a substantial loan within 10 years prior to the beginning of the recession. Such a modest pardon would help responsible individuals receive loans at a lower rate. The reason I only request a moderate bump in credit scores is that it helps the loaning party to differentiate between reckless individuals and relatively stable households. I understand that this is likely to be a pipe dream, but it is essential to highlight how the falling credit of the average individual threatens future economic growth.

For most of these proposals, their potential benefits are dulled due to the fact that most of the damage has already been done. However, it would be unwise to ignore the plight that many households faced due to the downturn. The law stands between aggressive and abusive practices by loaning agencies and households who were shaken by factors outside of their control. In addition, should another housing crisis strike the financial sector once again, it may be useful to have these proposals on the table.

Tuition Turmoil

Empirically, the value of a four-year college education increases the value of one's annual pay by thousands of dollars.[12] In addition, each extra year of education a student receives further increases his or her potential income. As the most recent recession destroyed millions of low-skill jobs, young individuals have flocked to universities hoping that their potential for employment will increase once they leave the institution.

Unfortunately, the cost of pursuing higher education has spiked over the past few decades. While the benefits gained still outweigh the costs of attending a university or college, it is becoming increasingly difficult for a student from a middle-class family to obtain an undergraduate degree.[13] If this trend continues, only well-off children will be able to afford these institutions, which worsens income disparity in the long-term.

There is no singular reason as to why the cost of a college education is rising, but there are several factors that contribute to tuition increases. Most jobs offering decent pay in the post-recession economy require a college degree or higher, and so the demand to attend these institutions has risen substantially.[14] Lower-income applicants are given the opportunity to apply for a variety of need-based grants and loans. However, colleges that offer generous scholarships pass the costs on to other students. Unfortunately, this places middle-income families who don't qualify for need-based scholarships in an uncomfortable situation.

In addition, most universities are in a state of expansion to accommodate higher enrollment rates. This requires a significant investment in new facilities, professors, administrative staff, dormitories, scholarships, and marketing to maintain the institution's reputation.[15] To cover these costs, colleges raise tuition rates for students currently attending. Universities hope that, over time, the demand for higher education will reach a plateau, which will allow them to refrain from increasing tuition costs.

While greater profit margins and endowments may appear to be a strong motive in raising the costs of a college education, this alone does not account for tuition hikes. Many public universities have their funds set by the state governments that run them, and most states have been cutting their expenditures for education.[16] Non-profit universities are required by law to publicly disclose their spending and income in great detail, and high salaries for the university administration invite nothing but criticism from the community. For-profit institutions are most likely to have profits in mind when raising tuition, but the other factors listed above play a greater role in determining the costs of education.

Fortunately, there are signs that the rapid rise in tuition may be slowing down. Recent data shows the slowest increase in tuition costs in over three decades.[17] It also indicates that enrollment numbers overall are starting to reach a peak. However, this does not mean that college will suddenly become more affordable. There needs to be new policies set in place to ensure that individuals who want an education will not be sucked into a debt vortex.

The most promising development in tackling rising tuition is that Congress and the Obama Administration enacted a law (the Health Care and Education Reconciliation Act of 2010) that makes it easier for students to pay their bills over time.[18] Student loan payments cannot exceed 10% of a student's initial income, and debt after 20 years of payment will be erased entirely. These are small steps that protect students during normal economic times, but these individuals may need more help in the event of another economic calamity.

Since education is an expensive and important investment, it is unlikely that college will return to an affordable range anytime soon. However, through effective regulation and reform, it is possible to ensure that student loans will be similar in structure to a mortgage for a car or home. In addition, we will likely see more parents realize the importance of sending their child to college, and save a portion of their money earlier to ensure their child is able to attend an undergraduate institution. Some states have implemented pre-paid college programs, which can pay for a substantial portion of all college bills if the parents start contributing to it early on.

Runaway Debt: Because We're Worth It

We have covered private debt up to this point, but have yet to focus on the growing spending of the federal government. As a progressive who views the government as a caregiver for the poor and disadvantaged, my instinctual reaction to massive government deficits and debt is to defend what that money has given us. If it were not for these investments, we would face a difficult moral and economic dilemma, as the care for these individuals would be the responsibility of the private sector. This would result in a massive capital drain for households, and the potential for fraud and abuse would grow astronomically.

However, even I must admit that the growing debt and high budget deficits are something worth capping. The actual debt is calculated and maintained by the US Treasury, but it is impossible to gauge at one particular point in time. However, the current estimates by various sources suggest that we owe close to 13 trillion dollars to other governments and private institutions, a number that is mind-numbing to comprehend.[19] If one includes obligations such as Social Security payments, that number increases to about 17 trillion dollars.

Before moving on, I feel the need to explain the difference between US budget deficits and US debt. Despite being incredibly simple concepts, there are too many commentators who complain about one or the other without a clear understanding of either. When policymakers discuss the federal deficit, they usually refer to the budget set by Congress. The federal government currently spends more money than it receives, which is signified through the budget deficit. To cover the costs of current federal programs, the Treasury is authorized to issue US debt to foreign governments or private parties. Most of the budget talks are aimed at reducing or eliminating the deficit, which results in less debt accumulating over time.

The good news is that the United States, thus far, has faithfully paid for all of its obligations, maintaining confidence in the parties that purchase US bonds. However, having the debt double in the last 10 years is a startling fact to consider, and may deter these parties from loaning any further.[20] Having the United States default on its debt would literally destroy the global economy, as investors would find the largest economy in the world untrustworthy to do business with.

The prime cause of high US debt stems from a few key decisions. President Reagan dramatically increased the size of defense spending while simultaneously pushing for tax cuts, under the assumption that Congress would have no choice but to cut or eliminate discretionary and safety net programs. However, this did not happen, and the debt levels continued to rise throughout the first President Bush's term. President Clinton, through compromises with the Republican Congress, saw the deficit decline substantially, which initially signaled the end of skyrocketing debt. However, his successor, President George W. Bush, enacted tax cuts and greatly increased defense and other spending in response to the September 11th attacks. Once President Obama came into office, he enacted several spending plans to counteract the effects of the recent recession.

It is important to note that the funds spent during the later Bush and early Obama years were necessary expenditures. The federal government needed to respond to the recent recession quickly, which lead to high emergency deficit spending. Trying to maintain a balanced budget during depressed financial times is self-defeating.[21] Not only will the demand for government services rise dramatically, but the amount of tax revenue will quickly drop due to depressed incomes.

Thus, the federal government is now facing one of the greatest challenges of the developed world. The process of significantly shrinking government expenditures is a painful pill to swallow, and has led to turmoil in European countries that suffered from overspending.[22] However, because the United States government has firm control over the spending of its agencies, we should have an easier time than our counterparts in Greece and Spain. I hope.

How To Earn 1 Trillion Dollars In 6 Easy Steps

The primary step to solving the current fiscal situation is a thorough examination of the current federal budget. As of print, the budget consists of a few prime categories of spending: Defense, Medicare and Medicaid, Social Security, Interest on Debt, Safety Net, and Discretionary.[23] Breaking these down individually will show the prime challenges facing the federal budget.

Defense spending is approximately 20% of our current expenditures. This is predominantly due to our previous involvement in two wars and the fact that we supply arms and other military support to allies around the world. While there is no doubt that the defense budget is filled with extraneous and unnecessary projects, reducing the size of this slice of the pie is difficult. The political will to cut defense spending is only favored by a minority of Congress, one that is not smoothly split along party lines. Also, the vast majority of budget experts and policymakers have limited insight into where taxpayer money is spent, due to the need to keep certain programs classified. Despite these longstanding challenges, the Pentagon and the Obama administration have recently proposed a substantial cut to the defense budget.[24] Policymakers are warming up to the idea that reduced military spending will not compromise national security.

Medicare and Medicaid are the fastest growing obligations of the federal government. The Affordable Care Act has expanded the coverage of individuals eligible for Medicaid, and it is likely that federal and state governments will be seeing a growth in health care expenditures in the short term. For Medicare, the Baby Boom generation (those born between 1946-1964) will be signing up for Medicare en masse, and politicians seeking to curb spending will face the onslaught of the new elderly. The key to reducing spending in this sector is to cap health care costs as a whole. There is an entire chapter in this book dedicated to that single goal.

The problems plaguing Social Security, the program that assists elderly Americans after they reach a certain age, stem from a lack of foresight from the policymakers that set it up. Demographic shifts, falling revenues, and a wave of new recipients are beginning to drain a once self-sufficient system.[25] The funds used to pay for Social Security are expected to run out by 2033, after which the government will have no choice but to raise taxes or reduce spending on it entirely.[26] There are many proposals to increase funds or reduce costs for this program, but none have yet to gain strong support.

"Interest on debt" is self-explanatory, as it accounts for the portion of the budget used to pay off obligated debts. Currently, this category is not a significant amount of federal expenditures. However, if the debt levels continue to rise, the funds used to maintain our credit will eat up a larger portion of our budget overall. There is nothing policymakers can do to adjust this growth without eliminating the budget deficit first.

Safety net programs are used to care for Americans who need temporary assistance. This includes unemployment, welfare, food stamps, disability benefits, and other programs that help disadvantaged individuals.

Many conservatives seek to reduce these programs, as they see them as a means for people to take advantage of government funding without providing productive work.

However, these programs are actually a means of promoting economic activity and employment, and some people rely on them to enter the job market.[27] This category is unlikely to substantially shrink without negative consequences for those who the program was intended to help in the first place. The best way to reduce the size of these safety nets will not come from spending cuts alone, but instead by encouraging employers to hire individuals who would be affected by the loss of these programs.

Discretionary spending is the category that often receives the most scrutiny. The spending devoted to maintaining the federal bureaucracy is a favorite target for small government advocates, as it resembles a behemoth that must be tamed. However, the programs that are often blamed as "wasteful spending" make up a tiny portion of the budget altogether.[28] Although efforts to ensure efficiency in these programs are valiant, policymakers should spend most of their time on other categories first, such as Medicare and Social Security.

The 535 Budgeteers!

Clearly, the challenge of reducing the federal budget to manageable levels is an arduous task, one that will literally require the nation to reconsider its priorities. Are elderly Americans willing to sacrifice some of their comfort to ensure the longevity of programs such as Medicare and Social Security for generations to come? Can we accept reducing programs that the poor rely on to survive? Will cutting defense spending put our nation at risk of attack? These questions will be answered in the coming decades, and only voters are able to determine how cutting spending will improve our budget.

One of the most promising developments has been the formulation of several budget deals. After months of partisan gridlock and the government shutdown, both parties are beginning to work on evaluating federal spending. In addition, Congress and President Obama are considering a revision of the tax code, which could improve efficiency in tax collecting and increase revenue without burdening middle class households.[29]

Debt can be considered all the weight on board our capitalist ship. If the load it carries is too heavy, our journey could face significant delays or steer off course. Policymakers must understand that although the threat of our financial obligations is passive, it can compromise the growth that we have achieved thus far. Sovereign debt will be one of the defining challenges of the 21st century, as developed governments consider how to pay for necessary projects and programs.

Chapter 10

Income Inequality

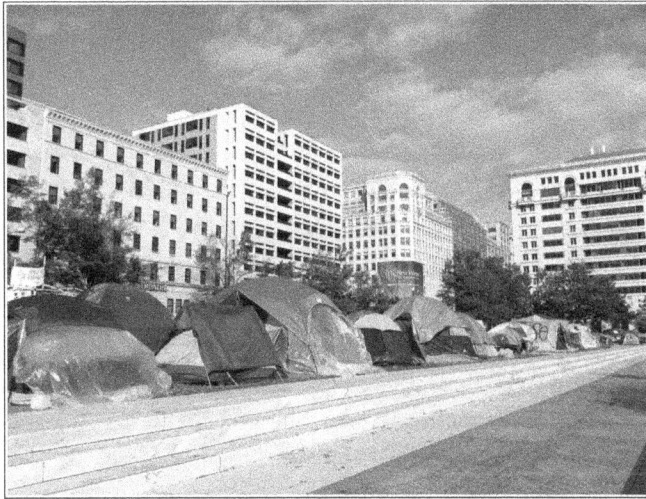

Occupy DC camp at Freedom Plaza, October 21, 2011

DECEMBER 18TH, 2011, WAS A CHILLY EVENING, and I was walking around the downtown area of Washington, DC. I was getting ready to leave, but a group of tents caught my eye. I had seen the protesters and camps on television in New York, Los Angeles, and other metropolitan areas, but I had not seen them in person. Considering that most cities were beginning to tear down the settlements, and that DC was almost certainly going to do the same, I decided to see the "Occupy Wall Street" movement with my own eyes.

At the time, two camps were set up in our nation's capital: one in Freedom Plaza, and one in McPherson Square. In Occupy DC's prime, hundreds of people would congregate in these public spaces daily to coordinate their campaigns and protests. Yet, by the time I arrived at the camps, only a handful of political activists remained, along with a few dozen homeless people. Although the camp was remarkably clean, the signs of sanitary decay were obvious.

I only had the opportunity to converse with a few of the organizers. They told me that the beauty of this movement was that every voice was welcomed, so long as it contributed to the community. I completely sympathized with the message Occupy initially conveyed. The United States has one of the highest rates of economic inequality amongst the developed countries, and shows no strong signs of improving.[1]

However, as I left the camp that night, I felt the same ambivalence the rest of the American public had regarding the movement. What Occupy gained in public sympathy and support was lost in its lack of leadership, incoherent messages, incredibly short-term planning, and infiltration of radical ideologies. Eventually, the authorities removed all camps, leaving the Occupy movement to fall into political limbo.

While the Occupy Movement failed to manifest into powerful political action, it did succeed in drawing national attention to rising income disparity. The divide between rich and poor has become a prominent concern for politicians and the media.[2] The public is becoming increasingly aware of the influence money has on the political process, and fears that its views are being shut out in favor of large donors.

This chapter focuses on the issue of income inequality in the United States, which has surfaced within the past few decades. It has become more apparent that the current trend of growing income divisions will cause economic and political dysfunction in the near future. By focusing on the root of inequity and examining potential policy options, we could mitigate growing income disparity without severely hindering incentives for financial success.

Let Them Eat High Fructose Corn Syrup

Until recently, income inequality had been a passing concern for economists. Allowing wealth to accrue amongst affluent individuals is beneficial to the economy overall, as long as their money is used to advance new projects.[3] More investment leads to more workers being hired, which has a cascading effect on promoting economic activity amongst middle class households. Thus, high taxes and restrictions on wealth accumulation would inevitably discourage growth, which could lead to recessions or reduce wages overall.

Large companies often pay high-level executives ludicrous salaries, which are, on average, hundreds of times more than the income of a middle class worker.[4] Outside of the business world, such compensation makes no sense, since the labor they provide does not equate to the wage they receive. However, it is important to remember that management and leadership are particularly valuable skills, and companies seek the best executives to lead their company. Exorbitant salaries encourage loyalty for these individuals, and prevent other corporations from stealing the top talent.[5] Theoretically, the profits generated from having a good chief executive greatly outweigh the costs of retaining such talent.

In a perfect market, this disparity would pose no threat to the economy, and would eventually be balanced out due to Adam Smith's concept of the "invisible hand." Since most of the money being spent by the rich stimulates the economy, middle class incomes rise along with the wealthy.[6] In addition, the "comfortable" lifestyles of the rich encourage middle class entrepreneurs to work hard, innovate, and increase their own income. During normal and prosperous economic times, it seems as if the assumption of wealth "trickling down" is correct, and plays a dominant role in determining income and tax policies.

However, the 2008 financial crash and its aftermath revealed a darker truth. While the incomes of the wealthy have skyrocketed since the recession ended, middle and lower class wages have remained stagnant, with no signs of increasing in the short-term.[7] The financial sector is stronger and richer than ever, but growth in other important sectors has stalled. Despite record profits at some of the top companies, unemployment remains stubbornly high.

There is a growing body of research that highlights the dangers of allowing high-income inequality to continue.[8] Wealth disparity in and of itself poses no threat to our financial and social systems, but the long-run side effects of ignoring the plight of middle and lower class households can stagnate future economic growth. We will now explore some of these consequences, and consider potential remedies to this situation.

Random Income Generator

The concept of the American Dream assumes that anyone, regardless of economic or social background, can achieve success through hard work and good financial planning. While being born into wealth may improve one's chance of success, middle and lower class individuals can still move up the social ladder. However, the United States actually has some of the lowest socioeconomic mobility in the developed world, a trend that widens over time.[9]

There are those who take the mantra of "hard work equals success" to the logical extreme, and reverse it to explain why many in this country are impoverished. This mindset assumes that poor individuals are suffering because they made bad personal decisions at some point in their life. Whether the person dabbled in criminal activity, dropped out of school, or was just outright lazy, there were more than enough opportunities to escape poverty outright.[10]

According to this viewpoint, the best way to lift people out of poverty is to simply motivate them to find good work. They assume that social services such as welfare discourage attempts to seek a job. Thus, tying these benefits to finding work or eliminating them outright will encourage most poor people to become involved in productive labor. The idea that the poor "reap what they sow" dominates the conservative political landscape, and motivates most attempts at reducing government services.

However, this assumption no longer stands firm, as evidence points to external sources of poverty. Most impoverished individuals ended up in their position due to decades or centuries of discriminatory policies and practices.[11] To make matters worse, ill-conceived policies contributed to the division between rich and poor by only favoring the highest paid households. As a result, rising income inequality perpetuates the sub-par conditions that many lower-income families face.

It is shocking to learn how difficult it is for people in poverty to access services that could help them find decent employment.[12] Many lower-income adults make their living by working long hours at a lackluster job, which often pay minimum wage salaries. Most of the money they earn is used to feed and shelter their families or pay bills and debts. What little spare time they have is spent caring for their children or other relatives, leaving no room for higher learning or searching for better employment.

Outside of personal matters, those in poverty are living in locations that make it difficult for them to prosper. High crime is rampant in their neighborhoods, where a lack of trust between police and local residents hinder crime prevention.[13] In addition, these areas tend to be most prone to environmental pollution, and suffer debilitating health care costs due to unsafe conditions. While one could argue that these individuals should simply live in another location, it is impossible for low-income families to afford suitable living spaces.[14]

The argument that poor people don't work hard enough fails to account for any of these dilemmas, and often leads to counterproductive policy decisions. The combination of budget cuts to public assistance programs and an ultra-competitive job market condemn lower-income households to a life of stagnancy.[15] Instead of shaming people for being in an uncontrollable situation, anti-poverty measures should assist those in need by making it easier to access services necessary to become a competitive worker.

One of the first steps to reduce income inequality is to dismantle the false assumption that poor individuals deserve their status. Social factors play a far greater role in maintaining poverty than the personal decisions of these households. Correcting these conditions will not only improve the lives of impoverished families, but also allow them to increase their productivity and chances of success.

Regular Versus Premium Learning

The greatest tragedy over the past few decades is inequality in access to a decent education system. While the children of wealthy families enjoy opportunities to attend top-performing schools, poor and middle-class households are receiving inadequate public education. It is well known that comprehensive schooling is the greatest factor in propelling someone from poverty to the middle class.[16] Unequal access to a proper learning experience is a dangerous trend, as employment prospects that do not require higher education are rapidly disappearing.

A high school diploma, a milestone that almost every American can afford, is no longer the threshold for a middle class worker. Higher education is a premium that is becoming harder for middle and lower class individuals to obtain.[17] While there are scholarships available that provide need-based financial aid for a college education, they do not amount to anywhere near the rising costs of tuition.

The last economic downturn further complicated this conundrum by destroying well-paid jobs held by undereducated workers. Many middle class laborers were laid off once the recession took hold, and many of the jobs lost have either been automated or have become obsolete.[18] The only available work for these individuals is low-paying positions, most of which offer no chance of advancing further.

The drastic difference in quality of public schools is partially responsible for our wealth disparity. A child from a well-off suburban neighborhood will almost always receive a different public education experience than a student living on the South Side of Chicago. By restricting the best schooling experience to children whose parents can afford the greater overall costs, the system inherently creates a dichotomy that handicaps middle and lower class families.[19]

The good news is that technological innovations provide many opportunities for poorer individuals to access adequate learning resources. There are many free or subsidized online programs that cover everything from introductory math to advanced linguistics. However, many schools serving low-income students and workers lag behind in adopting new technologies.[20] Hopefully, these changes will trickle down to all schools, allowing every citizen to take advantage of these resources.

Bad Risk Analysis Killed the Dinosaurs

We spent time discussing factors that are contributing to income inequality, but have yet to address the actual consequences of allowing such trends to continue. As stated earlier, wealth disparity is not harmful by itself, and currently does not have a significant impact on the nationwide economy. However, it is becoming increasingly apparent that the results of wide income gaps will damage future prosperity.

The main concern economists have regarding income inequality is how it affects socioeconomic mobility. In other words, analysts are considering how sizable wealth gaps impact the capacity for middle or lower class individuals to advance up the income "ladder." The most recent research concludes that, despite the rise in income inequality, there has been no change to overall economic opportunity in the past 30 years.[21]

However, the same group found that regions with high wealth inequity, such as the Southeastern states, have less mobility than those with smaller gaps in income.[22] The implications of this are important, as they prove a substantial link between hindered economic growth and strong class divisions. It's no coincidence that the states with the highest income gaps also have the worst marks for public education performance and access to health care.[23]

Speaking of health, the stagnant or diminishing wealth of middle and lower class neighborhoods poses dangerous scenarios for the quality of life in these regions. Because wealthy households are increasingly concentrated away from the general populace, there is less tax income available for these communities. Depressed incomes reduce tax expenditures overall, making it difficult for municipalities to maintain adequate services such as clean water, education, and park maintenance.[24] Over time, the general health of the community will decline, increasing health care costs in the region and reducing productivity overall.

We still do not understand the full impact of the most recent recession on wealth distribution, and how it affects the consequences of income inequality. The fallout from this crash has created a perfect storm that exaggerates the worst aspects of substantial income inequality, as the middle class gradually shrinks in size. Whether or not high-income earners can maintain their exponential growth, the economy will not benefit without improving the prospects for middle-wage workers.

Unfair Class Warfare

Let us suppose that our worst fears are realized, and greater income inequity creates stronger class divisions and less economic mobility. What will eventually occur will be the formation of a strong socioeconomic class system. The middle class, often seen as the baseline for a modest standard of living, would continue to shrink until people are roughly divided between lower and upper income brackets.

Outside of a moral dilemma, having extreme wealth gaps would be detrimental to economic growth. Without a plentiful supply of middle-income entrepreneurs to introduce new ideas, companies would fail to innovate further. In addition, lower wages with fewer opportunities for advancement would demote incentives for productivity.

The most detrimental outcome of an absolute division between rich and poor would be social and political instability. If our government almost always favors policies that aid the wealthy, those in lower-income brackets would lose trust in established institutions. Without widespread faith in the markets, economic growth would stall, increasing the likelihood of social unrest.

Fortunately, this grim prediction is unlikely to conform to reality.

Economics as a field highlights our selfish motivations, but it also implicitly recognizes our understanding of societal well-being. The market is only sustainable if everyone experiences improvements in the long run.[25] Thus, we can safely assume that we as a society will do everything we can to avoid this scenario.

Of course, this does not mean that the average individual or policymaker should not be concerned with uneven income distribution. Tackling this growing threat now would reduce or eliminate the damage income inequality would incur. Quick action would also minimize the burden on the government to care for impoverished households, and make it easier for the wealthy to adjust to new changes.

Legislation Conflagration

Currently, the federal government is shrinking many public services across the board in an attempt to control the budget deficit. One sector that should maintain adequate funding is the safety nets provided for lower income individuals. Without assistance, these individuals who cannot easily find respectable employment would be forced to fend for themselves. The only two options remaining for those reliant on these services is a life of crime or finding a family member who would take care of them. Both significantly dampen consumer spending, a necessary component for economic growth.

There are many options the government has to prevent income inequality from growing at a faster rate. The most straightforward action is to raise income taxes on those who make up the top bracket of wage earners, and use this revenue to improve impoverished communities. Progressives tend to favor this option, as it directly funds projects that provide assistance to disadvantaged individuals.[26] Conservatives clearly despise higher taxes, and believe that it unfairly punishes successful businesses and reduces job creation.[27]

Is the cost of taxing the wealthy greater than the benefits the poor will receive? The answer depends on who experiences the tax increase, how high the cost is for those paying it, and how those funds are being spent. If tax increases do not consume a significant amount of capital returns, there should not be any harmful repercussions to the economy in the long run.[28] However, if safety-net programs continue to experience budget cuts, income inequality would not lead to improved conditions for those in need.

Another major policy the government can implement is a higher minimum wage. As the term implies, increasing the base salary for the lowest paid positions would expand the purchasing power of these workers. Since most impoverished workers rely on low wages, increasing their income could provide disposable funds that could help lift them out of poverty.[29]

However, most minimum wage jobs are not intended to be long-term careers, and increasing it does little to address some of the core causes of poverty. In addition, raising the salaries of these positions could crowd out the market for new laborers looking for work experience. Many economists are hesitant to suggest arbitrary wage hikes, because it can disrupt the labor market if lower-level positions suddenly become highly attractive.[30] Raising the minimum wage would increase demand for these jobs, preventing those who need employment most from obtaining it.

One option that is being considered on a theoretical level is the adoption of a universal basic income. The premise of this idea is that every individual would receive a minimal income that covers basic food, housing, and other essential costs. While every citizen would get a baseline salary from the government, driven individuals would be free to obtain jobs to increase their wages. Many progressives find this idea attractive because it ensures the welfare of all citizens, and some conservatives approve of it because it eliminates many government agencies they view as wasteful or inefficient.[31]

The problem with this concept is that it assumes that the prime source of poverty is simply a lack of funds. In addition, implementing this program may encourage poor habits amongst potential workers, and would reduce incentives for hard work. This proposal would also require a complete societal overhaul, which takes decades or possibly centuries to occur. For now, this concept should remain within the realm of academia until a viable alternative emerges.

Fortune 300,000,000

The federal government, if willing, can address the issue of income inequality. However, the other major player necessary for reducing wealth disparity is the private sector. [32] The capacity of companies, private institutions, and well-off households to reduce income disparity is far greater.

In order for these groups to even the economic playing field, we must dispel the stigma against providing for poor households. Marginalizing or punishing impoverished households will not result in productivity gains, and will further fuel wage disparities. In addition, we should help individuals in need seek out government or non-profit services that could improve their well-being.

At this point, you are probably sick of hearing about how education is the greatest tool to combat poverty. However, increasing access to a well-rounded education is an essential method for lifting children from poor families out of poverty. To achieve this, the private sector should take advantage of rapid technological growth and give at-risk children access to premier learning programs.

Andrew Carnegie wrote about a concept known as the "Gospel of Wealth," which dictates that successful individuals have a moral obligation to provide for those less fortunate.[33] Attacking the rich for their success could potentially hinder economic growth, and we should avoid the temptation to call for greater controls on wealth accumulation. In return, the wealthy should use some of their funds to improve the lives of those who cannot access resources necessary for a decent wage and education. Not only will this serve to society's benefit, but would also encourage greater economic growth from a vibrant middle class.

Of all the threats our capitalist ship faces, income disparity is the challenge furthest away from our trajectory toward growth. However, as this storm approaches, we can navigate our economy away from a potentially disastrous predicament. Only through fast action will we be able to escape the worst of this calamity. Public understanding of this problem will allow the private and public sector to navigate our ship into calmer waters.

Chapter 11:

Resources and the Environment

Palm Beach County, FL, December 27, 2012

WETLANDS INITIALLY WERE ONE OF THE MOST unappealing ecosystems known to man. A hotbed for insects and a wide variety of dangerous creatures, people originally assumed that they held little economic value. For centuries, wetlands all over the United States were cleared and drained to make way for agriculture and housing communities to care for a growing population.

However, over the past century, scientists have discovered how essential the wetlands are to our well-being. The trees within this ecosystem slow down the rate at which floodwaters from storms flow by holding the soil in place, preventing a rapid deluge in the surrounding areas. Without the wetlands, the natural floods that periodically occur have nowhere to go, and thus end up submerging streets and homes.

In addition, scientists have discovered that wetlands can safely absorb a variety of toxic chemicals. Considered the kidneys of the ecosystem, they filter out pollutants that are hazardous to the surrounding areas.[1] Although the natural process of breaking down toxins is slower than more technological means, it may be cost-effective for society to preserve this habitat to mitigate the effects of harmful human activity.

This chapter makes the case that shifting toward a sustainable economy is essential to maintaining long-term growth. We will explore the economic arguments for and against protecting the environment, as well as consider the future of energy consumption. As scientific evidence details the consequences of maintaining our current consumptive habits, policymakers must plan to adapt to new ecological factors.

In addition, it is essential to understand how climate change will impact the world economy over the next century. As greenhouse gas concentrations continue to rise, natural disasters and adverse weather shifts will only become more common. It is likely that our leaders will have to make difficult decisions to ensure the stability of the market.

The unfortunate truth about this crisis is that even if we change our consumer behaviors immediately, it will be decades or even centuries before this trend can naturally reverse.[2] Global temperatures will still continue to rise until the concentration of greenhouse gases returns to lower levels. However, we may be able to adapt to these new conditions, if we choose to recognize them.

When students first learn about economics, they discover that the field is dedicated to "maximizing the utility of limited resources." While I could advocate for environmental protection on social and moral grounds, there is a strong argument that the markets would also benefit from maintaining a more sustainable lifestyle. Thus, we will focus exclusively on the effect environmental damage and climate change will have on the economy, and discuss ways to minimize potential damage.

Science Matters

Before going any further, I should emphasize that there is no empirical doubt that climate change is occurring. 97 percent of all climate scientists firmly believe that global warming is real, and meteorological data suggests that greenhouse gases are contributing to this situation.[3] In addition, human activity is playing a significant role in accelerating environmental decay.

Though there may be disagreements among scientists regarding the severity of the crisis, it is better to remain cautious and take steps towards adapting to a slightly warmer world. The steps necessary to combat climate change do not require a complete overhaul of our markets, and most action will inevitably occur within the private sector. Even if climate change is not as severe as originally thought, making progress toward a sustainable economy can only bring long-term benefits.

Despite widespread evidence, a stubbornly high portion of the populace does not consider climate change or other environmental calamities a threat.[4] This denial has been largely orchestrated by special interest groups seeking short-term profit gains by maintaining the status quo. In addition, almost all "research" published by climate change opponents originate from non-academic or ideologically aligned sources.[5]

Normally, having a minority group doubt the existence of scientifically proven phenomena would not serve as an obstacle for major policy changes. However, environmental policies directly impact the profit margins of some of the largest and most profitable companies in the world, and they have funneled enormous sums of money to spread misinformation regarding the validity of hard science.[6] To make matters worse, many politicians who are responsible for science and energy policy deny the existence of climate change, and intentionally serve on committees where any meaningful legislation must pass.[7]

The good news is that the vast majority of young voters believe in climate change, and want the government to take steps to address it.[8] If this generation continues to gain political momentum, the potential for breakthrough climate policies would be promising. Before stating how we can push for quick action, it is essential to understand what is causing such environmental damage.

Dirt Cheap Dirty Fuels

Ever since the beginning of the industrial revolution, the United States has relied heavily (or entirely) on fossil fuels such as coal, petroleum, and natural gas. Without these potent sources of energy, businesses would never have developed better technologies that allowed the United States to emerge as an economic powerhouse. We have also benefited from an abundance of natural resources, and the development of portable electricity has sparked advancements that would have been unforeseen decades prior.[9]

However, the burning of fossil fuels has harsh side effects on both humans and the environment. The pollutants it generates are hazardous to the public health, and are known to decrease the air quality of areas with high concentrations of fossil fuel emissions. Impaired air quality has clear economic repercussions, as urban residents suffer from unhealthy conditions. This will inevitably lead to more cases of temporary or chronic lung diseases, rising health care costs and reduce revenue due to lost work hours.[10]

It is not only the air we breathe that is impacted from fossil fuel consumption. The process of obtaining these resources consumes an ample amount of water, and burning them produces polluted or acid rain.[11] There are also many cases of compounds from coal, oil, and natural gas infiltrating local water supplies, which leads to expensive cleanup costs for both governments and the companies involved.

In addition, while technological developments have allowed us to extend the life of these fuels, the means to obtain them have become more difficult. Companies are attempting to drill in previously protected lands as well as the oceans to keep up with the energy demand.[12] These areas are one accident away from total ecological collapse, and would require ample amounts of resources to restore.

Regulations and better business practices, such as mandating filters in power plants and car engines, have effectively reduced many of the problems associated with burning these fuels. However, efforts to reduce environmental regulations will reverse the progress made over the past few decades. If these campaigns succeed, it would lead to a greater chance of environmental disasters.

Economic Energy Ethics

One of the original arguments against aggressive fossil fuel use is that we would eventually deplete this potent source of energy. Such a scenario would destroy economic growth, as limited electrical power would stifle innovation and create brutal conflicts with other nations. However, innovations in fuel efficiency and extraction have greatly increased the lifespan of these commodities, allowing it to last for several generations. In addition, our society has started to consume less electricity overall, as innovations reduce the energy demand of new technologies.[13] While our concern regarding the limited supply of fossil fuels has diminished, our reliance on dirty sources of energy has other important consequences for the economy.

The production of oil has increased over time, but commercial gas prices will be slow to decline.[14] Petroleum is used in a wide variety of applications and is difficult to replace. The market cannot easily substitute for oil-based products. In addition, social instability in countries with large oil supplies has led to greater fluctuations in gas prices. As a result, consumers have few options but to accept the higher prices (and lower disposable income) or attempt to reduce their consumption.

The coal industry has slowly diminished over the past few decades.[15] Though there is an ample supply of it in the United States and abroad, it is also the dirtiest and most inefficient fossil fuel. As a result, coal is subject to strict environmental and workplace safety regulations. Over time, the higher costs from complying with tougher guidelines have taken a toll on this behemoth of an industry. However, considering how harmful coal is to ecosystems and the public health, the economy sees positive prospects once this dirty fuel is laid to rest.

A rising star in the world of energy economics is natural gas, which has seen a significant price drop in the past few years.[16] It is recognized as the "cleanest" of the three fossil fuels in terms of greenhouse gas emissions. As a result, policymakers in both political parties consider natural gas a "transition fuel," supplying our country with energy as we move towards cleaner technologies such as solar and wind power.[17]

Some environmentalists concede that effectively regulated and monitored natural gas can benefit both the environment and the economy. However, the prime concern arises from the lackluster oversight of extraction and transportation methods. Scientists still do not fully understand the side effects of drilling for natural gas, and reports of ecological hazards range from delusional to highly credible.[18] In particular, the process of hydraulic fracturing (also known as fracking) has come under strict scrutiny, posing a significant threat to local groundwater if companies or governments fail to uphold safety regulations.

Black Gold Turns Brown

Fossil fuels contain high concentrations of carbon dioxide (CO_2) and other greenhouse gases such as methane. These compounds trap more of the sun's heat and energy in Earth's atmosphere, and are the prime cause of global warming. While there are natural sources that contribute to carbon in the atmosphere, human activity plays an important part in rising CO_2 levels.[19]

According to the Department of Energy, the United States had the fifteenth highest per capita carbon dioxide emissions in 2011.[20] While this seems like an arbitrary figure, when we multiply that number by over 300 million people the impact our country has on the climate becomes apparent. Americans released about 5.49 billion metric tons of carbon into the atmosphere in 2011 alone. Only China surpassed us in terms of CO_2 emissions, with an incomprehensible 8.71 billion metric tons released in just one year.

While socioeconomic well-being is the prime reason behind our carbon footprint, geography and culture also plays a significant role. The United States has heavily invested in technologies and products that make our lives more convenient, and does not critically consider the consequences of high electricity consumption. In addition, the size of the United States is so vast that businesses and individuals regularly travel extremely long distances.[21]

Most people in the United States use a car as their primary means of transportation, and our country has been designed to accommodate the vast fleet of automobiles. These vehicles rely on fossil fuels, and are a significant contributor to carbon emissions, second only to electricity consumption.[22] Abandoning our roads is nearly impossible without massive incentive shifts and better means of alternative transportation.

While the rest of the developed world aggressively pushed through public transportation programs, the United States remains focused on constructing multi-lane highways. Public transportation has been more of an afterthought, appearing only in cities and regions where too many vehicles can lead to serious congestion. Even if mass transit gained social traction, the cost to implement such programs in a country such as ours would be extraordinary.[23]

The good news is that advancements in fuel efficiency, along with urbanization, have led to an overall decline in CO_2 emissions. However, we still release ridiculous amounts of greenhouse gases into the atmosphere. Without strong measures to invest in alternative sources of energy, we will likely remain reliant on fossil fuels for the next several decades. Such reliance will inevitably have an impact on the economy as the effects of climate change take hold.

Property Rights and Wrongs

The problem with environmental damage in general is how it affects society beyond the source of degradation. Natural events such as strong winds and floods can easily transfer materials and chemicals from one region to another, regardless of the intent of property owners.[24] As a result, pollutants and other hazards can easily spread beyond the legal limits of the site where industrial activity is taking place.

This is why preventing and containing ecological accidents is so important to maintain economic stability. It is clear that cleaning up immediate environmental damage is the responsibility of the parties involved. However, in the aftermath of such disasters, it is not easy to hold these companies responsible. The legal system is currently not consistent when determining an adequate penalty for indirect harm. Impacted communities experience a substantial decline in productivity and output after an environmental disaster, and it is difficult for these areas to recover once the damage takes hold.[25]

Most of our nation's land has been cleared for business, agricultural, or residential purposes. However, a small yet significant portion is protected as nature preserves, and is left untouched and free from human intrusion. Maintaining this wilderness is not only beneficial for tourism and economic activity, but also serves as a hub of vital scientific research. Without protecting these areas from industrial activity, we may never have the opportunity to study ecosystems and further develop our understanding of biology, chemistry, and other natural sciences.

The concept that individuals or businesses have free reign to do what they desire on the property they own must be limited when it comes to activities that threaten the local environment. Boundaries established by municipalities are often designed to minimize interaction between industrial activities and households. However, they occasionally overlook ecological factors, such as river flow or frequent storms, which could spread dangerous materials to residential areas.

One phrase eco-activists tend to use is "environmental racism." The basic definition of this term is that businesses participating in ecologically damaging practices often base their facilities in politically underrepresented neighborhoods.[26] These communities tend to be mostly low-income households, and host many minority families. While it is impossible to prove any actual racist intent on the part of these companies, they have been known to contribute to the sub-par conditions plaguing these neighborhoods. Long-term exposure to hazardous chemicals increases the risk of chronic diseases, making it difficult for workers to provide stable and productive work.

The Storm Before the Hurricane

Climate change is a gradual process, but one that will literally alter the world we live in. In order to adapt to these new conditions, we must expect the worst-case scenario that could arise and plan accordingly. There will be many challenges affecting every sector of the world's economy, and failing to account for any of them could stagnate economic growth.

Typically, climate activists label stronger and more frequent hurricanes as the prime example of the consequences of global warming. While meteorologists and other scientists caution against assuming a causal relationship between hurricane strength and warmer waters, they assert that higher temperatures will lead to an accelerated water cycle.[27] This results in a greater frequency of severe weather, and will statistically increase the formation rate of more powerful tropical storms.

Speaking of water, government planners and businesses will soon have to adjust for greater fluctuations of rainfall. Certain parts of the United States, such as the East Coast, will experience more recurrent rainstorms and floods as a result of climate change.[28] Meanwhile, the Southwest will continue to experience continuous periods of drought and dryness, as desertification spreads throughout the area. Water resource issues will only continue to worsen, causing states and nations to fight over appropriate allocation. We may come to a point where we will have to transfer floodwaters via pipelines in some regions to urban areas surrounded by deserts as far as the eye can see.

There is also the issue of displacement from rising sea levels. Scientists predict that many parts of the United States and the rest of the world will be submerged under water, forcing millions out of their homes.[29] Cities like Miami, New York, and San Francisco are at risk of being partially submerged by the end of this century. If immediate action is not taken, states and the federal government will be forced to spend billions, if not trillions, of dollars to repair infrastructure lost under water.

Changes in the ecosystem will also significantly affect agricultural productivity. As climate patterns change over time, certain parts of the world may find that their crops, some of which have been growing for centuries, will no longer last due to these new conditions.[30] We will most likely see a rise in incidences of crop failures, which will have a dramatic impact on the worldwide economy, affecting both consumers and governments.

Agriculture is not the only sector that faces serious consequences as a result of climate change. As the potential for property damage from natural disasters rises, insurance companies are forced to drop coverage in high-risk regions, reducing their customer base. Sectors that rely upon predictably colder climates, such as tourism or sports, may see a decline in revenue as the average number of cold days decline. In addition, more frequent storms could cause delays in shipping and transportation, which indirectly stifles productivity in a wide range of sectors.[31]

The greater instability of the markets will lead to shrinking consumer and investor confidence. Cities and regions prone to natural disasters could see a gradual decrease in outside investment, as fewer firms would be willing to expend capital in such risky areas. In addition, a surge in severe storms will increase the likelihood of adverse supply shocks, as companies may see their factories or production fields wiped out instantaneously.

As the private sector suffers from the effects of climate change, governments will be forced to make uncomfortable decisions. More hurricanes and storms are almost guaranteed to increase expenditures for emergency relief, costing a significant sum for taxpayers. With the present fiscal restraint, we would be unable to maintain the government programs we have today while simultaneously covering the costs of restorations.[32]

Masters of the Earth

If we were any other species, our response to the changing climate would be to accept the losses that befall us. However, humanity has proven its mettle in overcoming nearly impossible challenges and adapting to new situations. The only way we can thrive in a warming world is if we act immediately to build a sustainable and resilient economy. We need not give up our capitalist principles to accomplish this, as our society offers great rewards for companies that develop the technologies needed to weather these changes.

First and foremost, the initial step to solving our environmental woes is to significantly reduce or eliminate fossil fuel consumption. This can be accomplished by incentivizing fuel-efficient or battery-powered automobiles, facilitating the growth of public transportation, and reducing the amount of power we consume on a regular basis. In addition, as solar and wind power becomes more cost efficient, private investment should trickle away from fossil fuel corporations and towards clean technology.

Economists argue that the best way to reduce fossil fuel use is through implementing a carbon tax.[33] These taxes play two roles: they discourage further investment in fossil fuels and other sources of greenhouse gases, and they often fund scientific research that ultimately improves the efficiency of renewable resources. Although support for such a proposal is hard to advocate for in this political atmosphere, it is one of the best ways to encourage the markets to move toward sustainable and renewable technologies.

Right now the oil, coal, and natural gas industry has waged a vigorous campaign against attempts to tackle climate change, making it difficult for politicians to support these actions. However, momentum is on the side of environmentalists, as more citizens, particularly young individuals, are becoming cognizant of the threats of environmental degradation. This is embodied in the recent movement to have universities completely divest from fossil fuels.[34] If our academic institutions successfully transition towards investing in cleaner technologies, it encourages the rest of the nation to do the same.

To tackle the issue of rising sea levels, governments should prepare areas most vulnerable to flooding and storm activity. Officials should rely on scientific predictions to adjust to changes in agriculture, living space, water resource distribution, and other impacted sectors. Our governments will serve as the first line of defense in the event of a major natural disaster. Having a plan to respond to climate change is the best service a government can accomplish today.

In addition, no country should exploit the regulatory differences between each other to earn additional revenue. Weaker environmental regulations in other nations may be what is best for them in the short term, but can have a worldwide impact that stifles economic growth in the long run. The Kyoto Protocol was an attempt to encourage governments to work together and implement similar rules. However, if we are to tackle global warming head on, environmental regulations and enforcement must be synced between countries.

We should prioritize building floodgates, levees, or other forms of flood mitigation as soon as possible to preserve some of our most economically essential cities. Alternatively, governments may have to look into the option of relocating residents who are at risk of losing their homes. Such an option may be unpopular and premature, but the cost of relocating can be far lower than the cost of rebuilding.

Climate change and environmental degradation are perhaps the biggest threats to our capitalist ship, and we cannot avoid these inevitable storms. However, with adequate preparations, we will not only overcome this hardship, but also use it to motivate us to create better technologies that place less pressure on the planet. The fate of our journey relies upon the actions we take today to transition towards sustainable economic growth.

Summary of Suggested Solutions

The general public must understand these economic and political challenges if it seeks to optimize our market system. Hopefully, this book has provided a clear and concise explanation of these complex issues. The first step toward improving economic growth is to apply this knowledge when discussing these topics with our friends, family, and co-workers.

The major changes necessary towards solving these problems will require significant support from voters and policymakers. To channel our frustrations and concerns into action, we must utilize our democratic process and support policies or politicians that advocate for rational and comprehensive proposals. In the private sector, we can also enact change by promoting companies or groups that follow the spirit of a competitive, sustainable market.

Below is a list of proposed economic or political solutions, organized by chapter.

Chapter 1: A Brief Explanation of American Capitalism

- Utilize principles of supply and demand to craft policy that minimizes disruptions in market equilibrium.

- Continue to safeguard property rights of individuals and businesses, but place limits on this protection if it stifles further innovation and creativity.

- Maintain competitiveness in all essential sectors by avoiding unnecessary regulations and intervene to break up potential monopolies.

- Work with other democratic capitalist countries to favor trade with nations or regions where corruption and politics will not significantly stifle productivity.

- Protect basic labor rights by punishing companies with a record of worker abuse.
- Develop market incentives (government or private) to encourage innovation in promising fields.
- Allow for regulations and laws to protect the public, but give companies the opportunity to protest or offer viable solutions.
- Account for non-economic factors, such as the environment, when making policy decisions.

Chapter 2: What Else is There?

- Refute any misconceptions regarding the true nature of socialism, communism, centralized states, and other market systems.
- Recognize the intent of communist or anarchist revolutions, and understand how they rise and collapse.
- Avoid the temptation of dogmatically following the doctrines of capitalist or non-capitalist markets.

Chapter 3: Recessions, Depressions, and Market Failure

- Understand the cause(s) of the Great Recession and the response to market failure.
- Recognize the government's partial role in the recovery after a significant market downturn.
- Develop a general policy plan to address inevitable drops in consumer spending and employment.
- Enact any necessary regulations that discourage high-risk behaviors and over-speculation.
- Give the Consumer Financial Protection Bureau effective powers

to protect consumers from exploitation during harsh economic times.

Chapter 4: Political Perspectives and Paralysis

- Vote!
- Recognize the principles surrounding progressive and conservative economic thought.
- Understand the political forces moving the Democratic and Republican Party.
- Foster policy discussions and debates between leaders from both sides.
- Encourage disclosure of large donations and industry affiliations.
- Remove the power of re-districting from politicians and place it in a non-partisan body.
- Amend the US Constitution to allow Congress to control excessive campaign spending.

Chapter 5: Unemployment

- Encourage employment through policy incentives for businesses that hire full-time workers.
- Provide educational opportunities for adults who lost their job during the recession.
- Encourage small business loans in key growth sectors.
- Extend unemployment benefits, then reform the program to provide more opportunities for job training.
- Protect intern rights through adequate labor safeguards.

Chapter 6: Education

- Increase the value of a high school diploma through

standardizing and updating curriculum.

- Address factors relating to poverty and its impact on educational success.
- Provide teachers incentives for using effective learning techniques.
- Utilize new technology to provide comprehensive educational tools and tutoring to lower-income students.
- Direct high schools to include college or workforce preparations.
- Reform public schools before pushing for greater private and charter education.
- Continue to push for Common Core standards, but ensure that funding is not directly tied to test performance success.

Chapter 7: Health Care

- Revise laws regarding drug patents and protections to accelerate approval, while maintaining proper evaluations for new medicines.
- Encourage hospitals to emphasize preventative care and direct non-emergency medical cases to less expensive walk-in clinics.
- Mitigate the primary care physician shortage through benefits and programs for medical students.
- Empower nurses to have a greater role in providing health care.
- Enact reasonable caps for medical malpractice payments, and consider other measures of tort reform.
- Retain or improve the Affordable Care Act, and maintain the individual mandate.

- Encourage states to adopt the health care insurance marketplace.
- Discourage unhealthy behaviors and practices, which reduce health care costs in the long run.
- Utilize new technologies to reduce office work and costs.
- Adopt a universal digital format to safely share medical information nationally and internationally.

Chapter 8: Money, Currency, and the Dollar

- Maintain current US monetary policy practices until economic circumstances change.
- Provide the Federal Reserve enough room to independently make decisions.
- Avoid the temptation to tie the US currency to commodities or other goods.
- Pay attention to other major currencies, such as the Euro, to avoid economic instability.
- Encourage financial institutions to increase financial privacy and security, especially against hackers and terrorists.
- Allow crypto-currencies to prosper, but adjust policies to ensure fraud and taxation issues are accounted for.

Chapter 9: Debt

- Protect households who suffered from severe financial debt as a result of the recession.
- Inflate the credit score for individuals who were directly impacted by the housing crisis.
- Attempt to reduce tuition inflation and student loan debt.
- Focus on reducing the budget deficit through increasing

revenues and evaluating major federal programs.

- Continue to downsize the defense budget and eliminate unnecessary projects.
- Adjust Social Security and Medicare to provide for the current generation of seniors while ensuring benefits for future generations.
- Consider streamlining discretionary and safety net programs, but do not attempt to significantly reduce expenditures.

Chapter 10: Income Inequality

- Recognize the political, social, and financial threat income inequality poses for economic growth.
- Dismiss the outdated image of "lazy, spoiled" poor individuals.
- Encourage states and municipalities to address chronic poverty.
- Ensure educational equality and opportunity in public and private schools.
- Consider incremental increases in the minimum wage.
- Revise the tax bracket so that higher wealth taxes only effect the ultra-wealthy.
- Protect safety net programs that are proven effective, and consolidate or restructure failing aid policies.
- Research the potential for universal basic income, but do not implement such a program until evidence is consistent with economic attitudes.
- Encourage private institutions and individuals to revitalize and invest in struggling communities.

Chapter 11: Resources and the Environment

- Acknowledge climate change and environmental degradation, and counter efforts to deny its existence.
- Control air and water pollution by maintaining or increasing emission standards for fossil fuels.
- Reduce electricity consumption.
- Allow for the decline of coal, and discourage efforts to drill for oil in sensitive areas.
- Update regulations on natural gas extraction and use.
- Enact restrictions and taxes on carbon emissions.
- Encourage public transportation and incentivize lower costs for building new transit.
- Fully fund research in renewable energy sources.
- Prepare for climate change-induced alterations in residential and agricultural areas.

The issues discussed in this book represent some of the most pressing threats to our economic prosperity. However, we have only covered the surface of a much deeper ocean. There will be many new challenges to the capitalist ship, some of which have yet to take form. It is up to you, dear reader, to keep the ship afloat, and set sail toward new horizons.

List of Cited References

Chapter 1

1. "GDP (current US$)." World Bank, 18 Dec. 2013. <http://data.worldbank.org/indicator/NY.GDP.MKTP.CD/countries/1W?display=graph>.
2. Pandika, Melissa. "A New Drug Problem: Not Enough of Them." *USA Today*. Gannett, 06 Mar. 2014. <http://www.usatoday.com/story/news/nation/2014/03/06/ozy-drug-shortage/6118051/>.
3. Tabuchi, Hiroko. "One Obstacle Won't Budge in Japan's Fight With Deflation." *The New York Times*. The New York Times, 31 May 2013. <http://www.nytimes.com/2013/06/01/business/global/in-japan-a-hard-to-budge-obstacle-looms-over-the-fight-with-deflation.html?_r=1&>.
4. Lubin, Gus. "Meet The 24 Robber Barons Who Once Ruled America." *Business Insider*. Business Insider, 20 Mar. 2012. <http://www.businessinsider.com/americas-robber-barons-2012-3?op=1>.
5. Reed, Brad. "Does the AT&T Breakup Still Matter 25 Years On?" *Network World*. N.p., 19 Dec. 2008. <http://www.networkworld.com/news/2008/121908-att-break.html>.
6. Kim, Donald D., Teresa L. Gilmore, and William A. Jolliff. "Annual Industry Accounts: Advance Statistics on GDP by Industry for 2011." *Survey of Current Business* 92 (May 2012):6-22. <https://www.bea.gov/scb/pdf/2012/05%20May/0512_industry.pdf>
7. Rollag, Keith. "Bureaucracy (Weber)." Babson College. <http://faculty.babson.edu/krollag/org_site/encyclop/bureaucracy.html>.
8. Christina D. Romer, "Business Cycles." *The Concise Encyclopedia of Economics*. 2008. Library of Economics and Liberty. <http://www.econlib.org/library/Enc/BusinessCycles.html>.
9. Frank, Robert H. "The Vicious Circle of Income Inequality." *The New York Times*. The New York Times, 11 Jan. 2014.

<http://www.nytimes.com/2014/01/12/business/the-vicious-circle-of-income-inequality.html?_r=0>.

10. Weisenthal, Joe. "We Love What Warren Buffett Says About Life, Luck, And Winning The 'Ovarian Lottery'" Business Insider, 10 Dec. 2013. <http://www.businessinsider.com/warren-buffett-on-the-ovarian-lottery-2013-12>.

11. Ropeik, David. "Risk Perception." *Soapbox Science*. Nature, 11 May 2011. <http://blogs.nature.com/soapboxscience/2011/05/11/risk-perception?WT.mc_id=TWT_NatNetNews>.

Chapter 2

1. Marx, Karl, Friedrich Engels, and Samuel Moore. "Chapter 1: Bourgeois and Proletarians." *The Communist Manifesto*. 1888. Print. <http://en.wikisource.org/wiki/Manifesto_of_the_Communist_Party/1>

2. Wilson, Woodrow. *Socialism and Democracy*. 22 Aug. 1887. <http://www.heritage.org/initiatives/first-principles/primary-sources/woodrow-wilson-on-socialism-and-democracy>

3. Marx, Karl, Friedrich Engels, and Samuel Moore. "Chapter 2: Proletarians and Communists." *The Communist Manifesto*. 1888. <http://en.wikisource.org/wiki/Manifesto_of_the_Communist_Party/2>

4. Peter Kropotkin, *Kropotkin's Revolutionary Pamphlets*. Roger N. Baldwin, editor. Vangaurd Press, Inc. 1927. <http://dwardmac.pitzer.edu/Anarchist_Archives/kropotkin/revpamphlets/toc.html>

5. Vanderschraaf, Peter (2006). "War or Peace?: A Dynamical Analysis Of Anarchy." *Economics and Philosophy*, 22, pp 243-279. <http://journals.cambridge.org/action/displayAbstract?fromPage=online&aid=452627>

6. Sommerville, J.P. "Hobbes' Politics." *Hobbes' Politics*. University of Wisconsin. Web. <http://faculty.history.wisc.edu/sommerville/367/367-092.htm>.

7. Ward, Dana. "Disillusions of Anarchy." Pitzer College. <http://dwardmac.pitzer.edu/classes/Anarchy/finalprojects/flores/anarchy.html>.

Chapter 3

1. Broda, Christian, and Jonathan Parker. "The Impact of the 2008 Tax Rebates on Consumer Spending: Preliminary evidence." *Northwestern University, July 29* (2008). <http://insight.kellogg.northwestern.edu/article/the_impact_of_t he_2008_tax_rebates_on_consumer_spending/>

2. Sahm, Claudia R., Matthew D. Shapiro, Joel B. Slemrod. "Household Response to the 2008 Tax Rebate: Survey Evidence and Aggregate Implications." National Bureau of Economic Research. Working Paper #15421. October 2009. <http://www.nber.org/papers/w15421>

3. Weisberg, Jacob. "What Caused the Crash? Let the Bickering Begin." *Newsweek*. IBT Media, 13 Mar. 2010. <http://www.newsweek.com/what-caused-crash-let-bickering-begin-70921>.

4. "H.R. 1424 (110th): Emergency Economic Stabilization Act of 2008." *GovTrack.us*. Civic Impulse, LLC, 3 Oct. 2008. <https://www.govtrack.us/congress/bills/110/hr1424>.

5. Denning, Steve. "Lest We Forget: Why We Had A Financial Crisis." *Forbes*. Forbes Magazine, 22 Nov. 2011. <http://www.forbes.com/sites/stevedenning/2011/11/22/5086/ >.

6. "Track the Money." Recovery.gov, June 2012. <http://www.recovery.gov/arra/Transparency/fundingoverview /Pages/fundingbreakdown.aspx>.

7. "Estimated Impact of the American Recovery and Reinvestment Act on Employment and Economic Output from October 2011 Through December 2011" Congressional Budget Office, Feb. 2012. <http://www.cbo.gov/publication/43013>

8. "The Distribution of Major Tax Expenditures in the Individual Income Tax System." Congressional Budget Office, 29 May 2013. <http://www.cbo.gov/publication/43768>.

9. Weil, Dan. "Finding a Small Business Bank Loan." Bankrate, 19 Nov. 2008. <http://www.bankrate.com/finance/personal-finance/finding-a-small-business-bank-loan-1.aspx>.

10. Clark, Patrick. "An Uptick in Small Business Loans from Big Banks." *Bloomberg Business Week*. Bloomberg, 12 Mar. 2013. <http://www.businessweek.com/articles/2013-03-12/an-uptick-in-small-business-loans-from-big-banks>.

11. Spence, Michael. "Globalization and Unemployment." Foreign Affairs, July-Aug. 2011.

<http://www.foreignaffairs.com/articles/67874/michael-spence/globalization-and-unemployment>.

Chapter 4

1. "The Court and Constitutional Interpretation." US Supreme Court. <http://www.supremecourt.gov/about/constitutional.aspx>.
2. Erdmann, Elizabeth A. "We the People: A Constitutional Debate Between the Federalists and the Anti-Federalists." Center for the Study of the Presidency and Congress. 2010. <http://www.thepresidency.org/storage/documents/Fellows2010/Erdmann.pdf>
3. "Moving America Forward - The Democratic Party Platform." Democratic National Committee, 2012. <http://www.democrats.org/democratic-national-platform#america-works>.
4. "Reforming Government to Serve the People." Republican National Committee, 2012. <http://www.gop.com/2012-republican-platform_Reforming/>.
5. Madison, James. "The Federalist No. 10." *Daily Advertiser* [New York] 22 Nov. 1787.
6. "The Dying Art of Legislating." The New York Times, 01 Mar. 2014. <http://www.nytimes.com/2014/03/02/opinion/sunday/the-dying-art-of-legislating.html>.
7. Moldoveanu, George, and Octavian Thor Pleter. "Shrinking Bureaucracy." *Theoretical and Applied Economics* 7.7 (512) (2007): 7-10. <http://www.store.ectap.ro/articole/229.pdf>
8. Blahous, Charles P., III, and Robert D. Reischauer. "A Summary of the 2013 Annual Reports." *Trustees Report Summary*. Social Security Administration, Mar. 2013. <http://www.ssa.gov/oact/trsum/>.
9. Shlaes, Amity. "Does Cutting Taxes Really Shrink Government?" *Marketplace*. American Public Media, 25 Apr. 2013. <http://www.marketplace.org/topics/economy/commentary/does-cutting-taxes-really-shrink-government>.
10. Feulner, Edwin J. "Why We Need Welfare Reform." The Heritage Foundation, 24 Feb. 2014. <http://www.heritage.org/research/commentary/2014/2/why-we-need-welfare-reform>.
11. Weller, Christian E. "10 Reasons Why Public Policies Rescued the U.S. Economy." Center for American Progress, 29 May 2012. <http://www.americanprogress.org/issues/economy/news/2012/05/

29/11593/10-reasons-why-public-policies-rescued-the-u-s-economy/>.

12. Gabriel, Trip. "Ohio Governor Defies G.O.P. With Defense of Social Safety Net." The New York Times, 28 Oct. 2013. <http://www.nytimes.com/2013/10/29/us/politics/ohio-governor-defies-gop-with-defense-of-social-safety-net.html>.

13. Montgomery, Lori. "Richest 20 Percent Get Half the Overall Savings from U.S. Tax Breaks, CBO Says." The Washington Post, 30 May 2013. <http://www.washingtonpost.com/business/economy/richest-20-percent-get-half-the-overall-savings-from-tax-breaks-cbo-says/2013/05/29/645f75c6-c894-11e2-9245-773c0123c027_story.html>.

14. Krugman, Paul. "Conservative Origins of Obamacare." *Conservative Origins of Obamacare Comments*. The New York Times, 27 July 2011. <http://krugman.blogs.nytimes.com/2011/07/27/conservative-origins-of-obamacare/>.

15. Binder, Sarah. "Congress in the Rearview Mirror." The Washington Post, 31 Dec. 2013. <http://www.washingtonpost.com/blogs/monkey-cage/wp/2013/12/31/congress-in-the-rearview-mirror/>

16. Summers, Lawrence. "When Gridlock Is Good." The Washington Post, 15 Apr. 2013. <http://www.washingtonpost.com/opinions/lawrence-summers-when-gridlock-is-good/2013/04/14/8bfeab9c-a3c3-11e2-9c03-6952ff305f35_story.html>.

17. "Americans Down on Congress, OK With Own Representative." Gallup, 9 May 2013. <http://www.gallup.com/poll/162362/americans-down-congress-own-representative.aspx>.

18. Plumer, Brad. "More and More Americans Are Feeling the Effects of the Sequester." *Wonkblog*. The Washington Post, 29 May 2013. <http://www.washingtonpost.com/blogs/wonkblog/wp/2013/05/29/more-americans-are-feeling-the-effects-of-the-sequester/>.

19. *Citizens United v. Federal Election Commission*, 558 U.S. 310 (2010).

20. Bernstein, Jonathan. "More Money Spent on Obama-Romney in 2012? That's the Good News...." The Washington Post, 2 July 2013. <www.washingtonpost.com/blogs/plum-line/wp/2013/07/02/record-money-spent-on-obamaromney-in-2012-thats-the-good-news/>.

21. Young, Lindsay. "Outside Spenders' Return on Investment." Sunlight Foundation, 17 Dec. 2012.

<http://sunlightfoundation.com/blog/2012/12/17/return_on_invest
ment/>.

22. Sullivan, Sarah, and Stanton Glantz. "The changing role of agriculture
    in tobacco control policymaking: A South Carolina case study." *Social
    Science & Medicine* 71.8 (2010): 1527-1534.
    <http://www.sciencedirect.com/science/article/pii/S0277953610005
    769>

23. Fell, James C., and Robert B. Voas. "Mothers against drunk driving
    (MADD): the first 25 years." *Traffic Injury Prevention* 7.3 (2006): 195-212.
    <http://www.tandfonline.com/doi/abs/10.1080/1538958060072770
    5#.Uzm9f14zh7w>

24. Domini, Amy. "Citizens United Is Bad for Business, Too." The Hill, 16
    July 2012. <http://thehill.com/blogs/congress-
    blog/campaign/238049-citizens-united-is-bad-for-business-too>.

25. Mann, Thomas E., and Norman J. Ornstein. *It's Even Worse than It
    Looks: How the American Constitutional System Collided with the New Politics of
    Extremism.* New York: Basic, 2012. Print.

26. Matthews, Dylan. "How Redistricting Could Keep the House Red for
    a Decade." *Wonkblog.* The Washington Post, 8 Nov. 2012.
    <http://www.washingtonpost.com/blogs/wonkblog/wp/2012/11/08
    /how-redistricting-could-keep-the-house-red-for-a-decade/>

27. Klein, Ezra. "House Democrats Got More Votes than House
    Republicans. Yet Boehner Says He's Got a Mandate?" *Wonkblog.* The
    Washington Post, 9 Nov. 2012.
    <http://www.washingtonpost.com/blogs/wonkblog/wp/2012/11/09
    /house-democrats-got-more-votes-than-house-republicans-yet-
    boehner-says-hes-got-a-mandate/>.

28. Mangu-Ward, Katherine. "Your Vote Doesn't Count." Reason, 3 Oct.
    2012. <http://reason.com/archives/2012/10/03/your-vote-doesnt-
    count>.

29. "Is It Irrational to Vote?" The Economist, 23 Oct. 2012.
    <http://www.economist.com/blogs/democracyinamerica/2012/10/p
    residential-election-0>.

30. Baker, Scott, Nicholas Bloom, Steven J. Davis, and John Van Reenen.
    "Economic Recovery and Policy Uncertainty in the US." Center for
    Economic Policy Research, 29 Oct. 2012.
    <http://www.voxeu.org/article/economic-recovery-and-policy-
    uncertainty-us>.

31. DuBois, Joshua. "Congress Can Become Civil and Productive If
    Moderate Voters Demand It." *The Daily Beast.* Newsweek, 28 Oct.
    2013.

<http://www.thedailybeast.com/articles/2013/10/28/congress-can-become-civil-and-productive-if-moderate-voters-demand-it.html>.

Chapter 5

1. Bernstein, Jared, and Dean Baker. "The Unemployment Rate at Full Employment: How Low Can You Go?" *Economix.* The New York Times, 20 Nov. 2013.
    <http://economix.blogs.nytimes.com/2013/11/20/the-unemployment-rate-at-full-employment-how-low-can-you-go/>.
2. Klein, Ezra. "Full Employment Gives People Jobs. But It Also Gives Them Power." *Wonkblog.* The Washington Post, 20 Dec. 2013.
    <http://www.washingtonpost.com/blogs/wonkblog/wp/2013/12/20/full-employment-gives-people-jobs-but-it-also-gives-them-power/>.
3. Looney, Adam, and Michael Greenstone. "Unemployment and Earnings Losses: The Long-Term Impacts of The Great Recession on American Workers." *The Hamilton Project.* Brookings Institution, Nov. 2011.
    <http://www.hamiltonproject.org/papers/unemployment_and_earnings_losses_a_look_at_long-term_impacts_of_the_gr/>.
4. Lazear, Edward P., and James R. Spletzer. "The United States Labor Market: Status Quo or A New Normal?" National Bureau of Economic Research. Working Paper #18386, Sept. 2012. <http://www.nber.org/papers/w18386>.
5. "Employment Situation Summary." U.S. Bureau of Labor Statistics, 7 Mar. 2014.
    <http://www.bls.gov/news.release/empsit.nr0.htm>.
6. "Alternative Measures of Labor Underutilization." U.S. Bureau of Labor Statistics, 7 Mar. 2014.
    <http://www.bls.gov/news.release/empsit.t15.htm>.
7. "Employment and Unemployment Among Youth Summary." U.S. Bureau of Labor Statistics, 20 Aug. 2013.
    <http://www.bls.gov/news.release/youth.nr0.htm>.
8. Allan, Nicole. "Where the Recession Hit Us Hardest: An Interactive Map." *The Atlantic.* Atlantic Media Company, 20 Mar. 2013.
    <http://www.theatlantic.com/magazine/archive/2013/04/where-the-money-went/309269/>.

9. Hamilton, Walter. "Great Recession Has New Wrinkles for Older Workers." Los Angeles Times, 10 Nov. 2013. <http://articles.latimes.com/2013/nov/10/business/la-fi-older-jobs-20131110>.

10. Plumer, Brad. "How the Recession Turned Middle-class Jobs into Low-wage Jobs." *Wonkblog*. The Washington Post, 28 Feb. 2013. <http://www.washingtonpost.com/blogs/wonkblog/wp/2013/02/28/how-the-recession-turned-middle-class-jobs-into-low-wage-jobs/>.

11. Daley, Mary C. "The Great Recession: Part One." Federal Reserve Bank San Francisco, 30 May 2012. <http://www.frbsf.org/education/teacher-resources/economics-in-person/great-recession-part-one>.

12. "Job Openings and Labor Turnover Survey." U.S. Bureau of Labor Statistics, 11 Mar. 2014. <http://www.bls.gov/jlt/>.

13. "Which States Will Generate Jobs in 2014?" *Stateline*. The Pew Charitable Trusts, 7 Jan. 2014. <http://www.pewstates.org/projects/stateline/headlines/which-states-will-generate-jobs-in-2014-85899531072>.

14. "Employment Status of the Civilian Population 25 Years and over by Educational Attainment." U.S. Bureau of Labor Statistics, 7 Mar. 2014. <http://www.bls.gov/news.release/empsit.t04.htm>.

15. Waldron, Travis. "Government Job Losses Still Plaguing Economic Recovery As More Furloughs, Cuts Loom." *ThinkProgress*. Center for American Progress, 25 Mar. 2013. <http://thinkprogress.org/economy/2013/03/25/1769531/public-sector-job-loss/>.

16. Hartman, Mitchell. "When Unemployment Runs out -- What's Next?" *Marketplace*. American Public Media, 31 May 2012. <http://www.marketplace.org/topics/economy/when-unemployment-runs-out-whats-next>.

17. Williams, Roberton. "The Numbers: What Are the Federal Government's Sources of Revenue?" *Tax Policy Center*. Urban Center and Brookings Institution, 13 Sept. 2011. <http://www.taxpolicycenter.org/briefing-book/background/numbers/revenue.cfm>.

18. Blahous, Charles P., III, and Robert D. Reischauer. "A Summary of the 2013 Annual Reports." Trustees Report Summary. Social Security Administration, Mar. 2013. <http://www.ssa.gov/oact/trsum/>.

19. Matthews, Dylan. "Introducing 'The Tuition Is Too Damn High'." *Wonkblog*. The Washington Post, 26 Apr. 2013. <http://www.washingtonpost.com/blogs/wonkblog/wp/2013/08/26/introducing-the-tuition-is-too-damn-high/>.

20. "How The $1.2 Trillion College Debt Crisis Is Crippling Students, Parents And The Economy." *Forbes*. Forbes Magazine, 07 Aug. 2013. <http://www.forbes.com/sites/specialfeatures/2013/08/07/how-the-college-debt-is-crippling-students-parents-and-the-economy/>.

21. Seligson, Hannah. "The Age of the Permanent Intern." Washingtonian, 6 Feb. 2013. <http://www.washingtonian.com/articles/people/the-age-of-the-permanent-intern/>.

22. Fox, Emily J. "Unpaid Interns Not Protected from Sexual Harassment." *CNNMoney*. CNN, 09 Oct. 2013. <http://money.cnn.com/2013/10/09/news/economy/unpaid-intern-sexual-harassment/>.

23. Taylor, Joe, Jr. "Should You Use Unpaid Interns." Time, 22 Feb. 2013. <http://business.time.com/2013/02/22/should-you-use-unpaid-interns/>.

24. Kelly, Brian. "The State of STEM and Jobs." U.S.News & World Report, 21 Sept. 2012. <http://www.usnews.com/news/articles/2012/09/21/the-state-of-stem-and-jobs>.

Chapter 6

1. Loveless, Tom. "The Peculiar Politics of No Child Left Behind." The Brookings Institution, Aug. 2006. <http://www.brookings.edu/research/papers/2006/08/k12education-loveless>.

2. "NCLB Steals Time from Teaching." *FairTest*. The National Center for Fair & Open Testing, Nov. 2006. <http://www.fairtest.org/nclb-steals-time-teaching>.

3. Duncan, Arne. "No Child Left Behind: Early Lessons from State Flexibility Waivers." Testimony. U.S. Senate Committee on Health, Education, Labor, and Pensions, Washington. 7 Feb. 2013. *Department of Education*. <http://www.ed.gov/news/speeches/no-child-left-behind-early-lessons-state-flexibility-waivers>.

4. Jehlen, Alain. "NCLB: Is It Working?" National Education Association, Feb. 2009. <http://www.nea.org/home/20755.htm>.

5. "Earnings and Unemployment Rates by Educational Attainment." *U.S. Bureau of Labor Statistics*. U.S. Bureau of Labor Statistics, 24 Mar. 2014. <http://www.bls.gov/emp/ep_chart_001.htm>.

6. "Increasing College Opportunity for Low-Income Students." The White House, Jan. 2014. <http://www.whitehouse.gov/the-press-office/2014/01/16/fact-sheet-president-and-first-lady-s-call-action-college-opportunity>.

7. Mervis, Jeffrey. "Obama Advisers Call for Greater Emphasis on STEM Education." *ScienceInsider*. Science Magazine, 2 Sept. 2010. <http://news.sciencemag.org/2010/09/obama-advisers-call-greater-emphasis-stem-education>.

8. "Public School Systems Spend More than $10,000 Per Pupil in 2008." US Census Bureau, 28 Jan. 2010. <http://www.census.gov/newsroom/releases/archives/education/cb10-96.html>.

9. Dwyer, Sarah B., Jan M. Nicholson, and Diana Battistutta. "Parent and teacher identification of children at risk of developing internalizing or externalizing mental health problems: a comparison of screening methods." *Prevention Science* 7.4 (2006): 343-357. <http://link.springer.com/article/10.1007/s11121-006-0026-5>

10. "High School Teacher: Job Overview." US News and World Report, 22 Jan. 2014. <http://money.usnews.com/careers/best-jobs/high-school-teacher>.

11. Guild, Pat B. "Diversity, Learning Style and Culture." Johns Hopkins School of Education, Oct. 2001. <http://education.jhu.edu/PD/newhorizons/strategies/topics/Learning Styles/diversity.html>.

12. Fisher, Kenn. "Building Better Outcomes: The Impact of School Infrastructure on Student Outcomes and Behaviour. Schooling Issues Digest." (2001). <http://eric.ed.gov/?id=ED455672>

13. Mohai, Paul, et al. "Air pollution around schools is linked to poorer student health and academic performance." *Health Affairs* 30.5 (2011): 852-862. <http://www.ncbi.nlm.nih.gov/pubmed/21543420>

14. Boser, Ulrich, and Chelsea Straus. "Why Too Many Schools Live in an Analog World, and What We Can Do About It." Center for American Progress, 10 Feb. 2014. <http://www.americanprogress.org/issues/education/news/2014

/02/10/82614/why-too-many-schools-live-in-an-analog-world-and-what-we-can-do-about-it/>.

15. Hennigan, Gregg. "Adoption of Technology in Education Is Slow and Uneven." The Gazette, 4 Mar. 2012. <http://thegazette.com/2012/03/04/adoption-of-technology-in-education-is-slow-and-uneven/>.

16. Horn, Michael. "The Counterproductive Attack on NYC's School of One." *Forbes*. Forbes Magazine, 13 Sept. 2012. <http://www.forbes.com/sites/michaelhorn/2012/09/13/the-counterproductive-attack-on-nycs-school-of-one/>.

17. Rhames, Marilyn A. "A Great Idea, but Not Just for the Rich." The New York Times, 5 Feb. 2014. <http://www.nytimes.com/roomfordebate/2014/02/05/virtual-school-on-snow-days/virtual-school-on-snow-days-is-not-just-for-the-rich>.

18. Young, Jeffrey R. "A Tech-Happy Professor Reboots After Hearing His Teaching Advice Isn't Working." *College 2.0*. The Chronicle of Higher Education, 12 Feb. 2012. <http://chronicle.com/article/A-Tech-Happy-Professor-Reboots/130741/>.

19. Jensen, Eric. "Chapter 2. How Poverty Affects Behavior and Academic Performance." *Teaching with Poverty in Mind: What Being Poor Does to Kids' Brains and What Schools Can Do about It*. Alexandria, VA: Association for Supervision and Curriculum Development, 2009. <http://www.ascd.org/publications/books/109074/chapters/How-Poverty-Affects-Behavior-and-Academic-Performance.aspx>.

20. Bleachfield, Kyle. "Discipline vs. Punishment." EdWeek, 26 Feb. 2014. <http://blogs.edweek.org/edweek/op_education/2014/02/discipline_vs_punishment.html>.

21. Barajas, Mark S. "Academic achievement of children in single parent homes: A critical review." *The Hilltop Review* 5.1 (2012): 4. <http://scholarworks.wmich.edu/hilltopreview/vol5/iss1/4/>

22. Ludwig, Jens, Greg J. Duncan, and Paul Hirschfield. "Urban poverty and juvenile crime: Evidence from a randomized housing-mobility experiment." *The Quarterly Journal of Economics* 116.2 (2001): 655-679. <http://qje.oxfordjournals.org/content/116/2/655.short>

23. Rich, Motoko. "Enrollment in Charter Schools Is Increasing." The New York Times, 13 Nov. 2012.

<http://www.nytimes.com/2012/11/14/us/charter-schools-growing-fast-new-report-finds.html>.

24. Haimson, Leonie. "Class Size Matters Executive: Funds Drained for NYC Public Schools Thanks to Charters." NY Daily News, 14 Jan. 2014. <http://www.nydailynews.com/new-york/funds-drained-article-1.1578760>.

25. Harvey, James. "Privatization: A Drain on Public Schools." *Educational Leadership* 69.4 (2012): 48-53. Dec. 2011-Jan. 2012. <http://www.ascd.org/publications/educational-leadership/dec11/vol69/num04/Privatization@-A-Drain-on-Public-Schools.aspx>.

26. Strauss, Valerie. "School Vouchers: Still a Bad Idea despite Indiana Court Ruling." The Washington Post, 26 Mar. 2013. <http://www.washingtonpost.com/blogs/answer-sheet/wp/2013/03/26/school-vouchers-still-a-bad-idea-despite-indiana-court-ruling/>.

27. Strauss, Valerie. "Eight Problems with Common Core Standards." The Washington Post, 21 Aug. 2012. <http://www.washingtonpost.com/blogs/answer-sheet/post/eight-problems-with-common-core-standards/2012/08/21/821b300a-e4e7-11e1-8f62-58260e3940a0_blog.html>.

28. "Read the Standards." *Common Core State Standards Initiative.* National Governers Association. <http://www.corestandards.org/read-the-standards/>.

29. Loveless, Tom. "A Progress Report on the Common Core." The Brookings Institution, 18 Mar. 2014. <http://www.brookings.edu/research/reports/2014/03/18-common-core-loveless>.

30. Herold, Benjamin, and Michele Molnar. "Research Questions Common-Core Claims by Publishers." EdWeek, 3 Mar. 2014. <http://www.edweek.org/ew/articles/2014/03/05/23textbooks_ep.h33.html>.

31. Duncan, Arne. "Parent Voices for World-Class Education." National Assessment Governing Board Education Summit for Parent Leaders. Washington. 13 Jan. 2014. *Department of Education.* <http://www.ed.gov/news/speeches/remarks-us-secretary-education-arne-duncan-national-assessment-governing-board-educati>.

32. Matthews, Dylan. "Teach for America Is a Deeply Divisive Program. It Also Works." *Wonkblog.* The Washington Post, 10 Sept. 2013.

<http://www.washingtonpost.com/blogs/wonkblog/wp/2013/09/10/teach-for-america-is-a-deeply-divisive-program-it-also-works/>.

33. Rivera, Carla. "Montessori Schools Look to Future." Los Angeles Times, 30 Apr. 2007.
<http://articles.latimes.com/2007/apr/30/local/me-montessori30>.

Chapter 7

1. "History of Health Insurance Benefits." Employee Benefit Research Institute, Mar. 2002.
<http://www.ebri.org/publications/facts/index.cfm?fa=0302fact>.

2. Appleby, Julie. "Costs Of Employer Insurance Plans Surge in 2011." Kaiser Health News, 27 Sept. 2011.
<http://www.kaiserhealthnews.org/stories/2011/september/27/employer-health-coverage-survey-shows-employer-spending-spike.aspx>.

3. "Health Expenditure, Total (% of GDP)." World Bank, 2014.
<http://data.worldbank.org/indicator/SH.XPD.TOTL.ZS>

4. "2012 Comparative Price Report." International Federation of Health Plans, 2013. <http://www.ifhp.com/market-intelligence/>.

5. Ryan, Mandy, et al. "Eliciting public preferences for healthcare: a systematic review of techniques." *Health technology assessment (Winchester, England)* 5.5 (2001): 1.
<http://www.ncbi.nlm.nih.gov/pubmed/11262422>

6. Warner, Gregory. "The Battle over Billing Codes." *Marketplace*. American Public Media, 10 Apr. 2012.
<http://www.marketplace.org/topics/life/health-care/battle-over-billing-codes>.

7. Young, Pierre L., and LeighAnne Olsen. *The healthcare imperative: lowering costs and improving outcomes: workshop series summary*. National Academies Press, 2010.
<http://www.ncbi.nlm.nih.gov/books/NBK53933/>

8. Munro, Dan. "Healthcare's Story Of The Year For 2013 - Pricing Transparency." *Forbes*. Forbes Magazine, 15 Dec. 2013.
<http://www.forbes.com/sites/danmunro/2013/12/15/healthcares-story-of-the-year-for-2013-pricing-transparency/>.

9. Roy, Avik. "Health Care and the Profit Motive." *National Affairs* 3 (2010).

<http://www.nationalaffairs.com/publications/detail/health-care-and-the-profit-motive>.

10. Clarke, Toni. "FDA's Shorter Approval Time for New Drugs Raises Questions." NBC News, 28 Oct. 2013. <http://www.nbcnews.com/health/health-news/fdas-shorter-approval-time-new-drugs-raises-questions-f8C11484613>.

11. "Pharmaceutical Industry." World Health Organization. <http://www.who.int/trade/glossary/story073/en/>.

12. Herper, Matthew. "The Truly Staggering Cost Of Inventing New Drugs." *Forbes*. Forbes Magazine, 10 Feb. 2012. <http://www.forbes.com/sites/matthewherper/2012/02/10/the-truly-staggering-cost-of-inventing-new-drugs/>.

13. Tulenko, Kate. "America's Health Worker Mismatch." The New York Times, 13 Sept. 2012. <http://www.nytimes.com/2012/09/14/opinion/americas-health-worker-mismatch.html>.

14. Kangovi, Shreya, et al. "Understanding why patients of low socioeconomic status prefer hospitals over ambulatory care." Web. *Health Affairs* 32.7 (2013): 1196-1203. <http://content.healthaffairs.org/content/32/7/1196.abstract>

15. Porter, Eduardo. "Health Care and Profits, a Poor Mix." The New York Times, 08 Jan. 2013. <http://www.nytimes.com/2013/01/09/business/health-care-and-pursuit-of-profit-make-a-poor-mix.html>.

16. Carrns, Ann. "A Quicker Trip to the Doctor, for Minor Ailments." The New York Times, 18 Dec. 2013. <http://www.nytimes.com/2013/12/19/your-money/a-quicker-trip-to-the-doctor-for-minor-ailments.html>.

17. "Trends." Urgent Care Association of America. <http://www.ucaoa.org/trends.php>.

18. "Urgent Care Fact Sheet." American College of Emergency Physicians. <http://newsroom.acep.org/index.php?s=20301&item=30033>.

19. Yee, Tracy, Amanda E. Lechner, and Ellyn R. Boukus. "The Surge in Urgent Care Centers: Emergency Department Alternative or Costly Convenience?" *Health Care Change*. Center for Studying Health Care Change, July 2013. <http://www.hschange.org/CONTENT/1366/>.

20. "Honesty/Ethics in Professions." Gallup, 5-8 Dec. 2013. <http://www.gallup.com/poll/1654/Honesty-Ethics-Professions.aspx>.

21. Mann, Denise. "Study Foresees Shortage of Primary-Care Doctors." *HealthDay*. U.S. News & World Report, 4 Dec. 2012. <http://health.usnews.com/health-news/news/articles/2012/12/04/study-foresees-shortage-of-primary-care-doctors>.

22. Shi, Leiyu. "Balancing primary versus specialty care." *Journal of the Royal Society of Medicine* 88.8 (1995): 428. <http://www.ncbi.nlm.nih.gov/pmc/articles/PMC1295294/>

23. Smith, Jacquelyn. "The Best- And Worst-Paying Jobs For Doctors." *Forbes*. Forbes Magazine, 20 July 2012. <http://www.forbes.com/sites/jacquelynsmith/2012/07/20/the-best-and-worst-paying-jobs-for-doctors-2/>.

24. "Advancing Primary Care." *Council of Graduate Medical Education*. Department of Health and Human Services, Dec. 2010. <http://ask.hrsa.gov/detail_materials.cfm?ProdID=4517>.

25. Spetz, Joanne, and Ruth Given. "The future of the nurse shortage: Will wage increases close the gap?." *Health Affairs* 22.6 (2003): 199-206. <http://content.healthaffairs.org/content/22/6/199.full>

26. "Malpractice Rates Plateauing." *Medical Economics*. Advanstar Communications, Inc., 25 Nov. 2011. <http://medicaleconomics.modernmedicine.com/medical-economics/news/modernmedicine/modern-medicine-feature-articles/exclusive-survey-malpractice->.

27. Taylor, Geoff. "Medical Malpractice Premiums in NYS and Sample Costs Elsewhere in the US." Excellus BlueCross BlueShield, 17 Oct. 2011. <http://www.health.ny.gov/health_care/medicaid/redesign/docs/2011-10-17_medical_malpractice_premiums.pdf>.

28. "Limit Medical Malpractice Torts." Congressional Budget Office, 13 Nov. 2013. <http://www.cbo.gov/budget-options/2013/44892>.

29. Sargent, Greg. "Americans Know There's No GOP 'alternative' to Obamacare." *The Plum Line*. The Washington Post, 26 Feb. 2014. <http://www.washingtonpost.com/blogs/plum-line/wp/2014/02/26/americans-know-theres-no-gop-alternative-to-obamacare/>.

30. Thoma, Mark. "The Economics of the Health Insurance Mandate." *Forbes*. Forbes Magazine, 02 July 2012. <http://www.forbes.com/sites/markthoma/2012/07/02/the-economics-of-the-health-insurance-mandate/>.

31. *National Federation of Independent Business, et al. v. Kathleen Sebelius*, 567 U.S. ___ (2012)

32. Lee, Emily O. "The Costs of Delaying the Individual Mandate." Center for American Progress, 20 Oct. 2013. <http://www.americanprogress.org/issues/healthcare/news/201 3/10/30/78415/the-costs-of-delaying-the-individual-mandate/>.

33. Feldman, Roger. "Quality of care in single-payer and multipayer health systems." *Journal of health politics, policy and law* 34.4 (2009): 649-670. <http://www.ncbi.nlm.nih.gov/pubmed/19633227>

34. Pho, Kevin. "How Not to Convince Doctors to Embrace Single Payer." *KevinMD.com*. MedPage Today, 1 Sept. 2011. <http://www.kevinmd.com/blog/2011/09/convince-doctors-embrace-single-payer.html>.

35. Martin, Anne B., et al. "National Health Spending In 2012: Rate Of Health Spending Growth Remained Low For The Fourth Consecutive Year." *Health Affairs* 33.1 (2014): 67-77. <http://content.healthaffairs.org/content/33/1/67.abstract>

36. Okike, Kanu, et al. "Survey Finds Few Orthopedic Surgeons Know The Costs Of The Devices They Implant." *Health Affairs* 33.1 (2014): 103-109. <http://content.healthaffairs.org/content/33/1/103.abstract>

37. "Administration Offers Consumers an Unprecedented Look at Hospital Charges." Department of Health and Human Services, 8 May 2013. <http://www.hhs.gov/news/press/2013pres/05/20130508a.html>.

38. Pho, Kevin. "Price Transparency Alone Won't Solve Our Health System's Ills." *KevinMD.com*. MedPage Today, 8 Jan. 2014. <http://www.kevinmd.com/blog/2014/01/price-transparency-solve-health-systems-ills.html>.

39. Rosenthal, Elisabeth. "Think the E.R. Is Expensive? Look at How Much It Costs to Get There." The New York Times, 04 Dec. 2013. <http://www.nytimes.com/2013/12/05/health/think-the-er-was-expensive-look-at-the-ambulance-bill.html>.

40. "What Are the Health Risks of Overweight and Obesity?" *National Heart, Lung, and Blood Institute*. National Institute of Health, 13 July 2012. <http://www.nhlbi.nih.gov/health/health-topics/topics/obe/risks.html>.

41. "FACT SHEET: Creating Health Care Jobs by Addressing Primary Care Workforce Needs." The White House, 11 Apr. 2012. <http://www.whitehouse.gov/the-press-office/2012/04/11/fact-sheet-creating-health-care-jobs-addressing-primary-care-workforce-n>.

42. Stewart, Bridget A., et al. "A preliminary look at duplicate testing associated with lack of electronic health record interoperability for transferred patients." *Journal of the American Medical Informatics Association* 17.3 (2010): 341-344.
<http://www.ncbi.nlm.nih.gov/pmc/articles/PMC2995707/>

43. Noffsinger, Richard, and Steve Chin. "Improving the delivery of care and reducing healthcare costs with the digitization of information." *Journal of Healthcare Information Management* 14.2 (2000): 23-30.
<http://www.ncbi.nlm.nih.gov/pubmed/11066646>

44. Trotter, Fred, and David Uhlman. *Hacking Healthcare*. Sebastopol, CA: O'Reilly Media, 2013.

Chapter 8

1. Murphy, Robert P. "Modeling Money." Library of Economics and Liberty, 4 Jan. 2012.
<http://www.econlib.org/library/Columns/y2012/Murphymoney.html>.

2. "Functions of Money." *The Economic Lowdown Podcast Series*. Federal Reserve Bank St. Louis.
<http://www.stlouisfed.org/education_resources/economic-lowdown-podcast-series/functions-of-money/>.

3. "Understanding GDP and How It Is Measured." Office of National Statistics, 23 Aug. 2013.
<http://www.ons.gov.uk/ons/rel/elmr/explaining-economic-statistics/understanding-gdp-and-how-it-is-measured/sty-understanding-gdp.html>.

4. Gobry, Pascal-Emmanuel. "All Money Is Fiat Money." *Forbes*. Forbes Magazine, 08 Jan. 2013.
<http://www.forbes.com/sites/pascalemmanuelgobry/2013/01/08/all-money-is-fiat-money/>.

5. Kenney, Caitlin, and Zoe Chace. "The Economic Catastrophe That Germany Can't Forget." National Public Radio, 14 Sept. 2011.
<http://www.npr.org/blogs/money/2011/09/14/140419140/the-economic-catastrophe-that-germany-cant-forget>.

6. Feige, Edgar L. "New estimates of US currency abroad, the domestic money supply and the unreported economy." *Crime, law and social change* 57.3 (2012): 239-263. <http://mpra.ub.uni-muenchen.de/34778/>

7. "Go with the Flows." The Economist, 20 Jan. 2011.
<http://www.economist.com/node/17956749>.

8. Tavlas, George. "The International Use of Currencies: The U.S. Dollar and the Euro." *Finance and Development* 35.2 (1998). International Monetary Fund. <http://www.imf.org/external/pubs/ft/fandd/1998/06/tavlas.htm>.

9. "The Federal Reserve's Dual Mandate." Federal Reserve Bank Chicago, 20 Mar. 2014. <http://www.chicagofed.org/webpages/publications/speeches/our_dual_mandate.cfm>.

10. Conerly, Bill. "Future Of The Dollar As World Reserve Currency." *Forbes*. Forbes Magazine, 25 Oct. 2013. <http://www.forbes.com/sites/billconerly/2013/10/25/future-of-the-dollar-as-world-reserve-currency/>.

11. Boesler, Matthew. "There Are Only Two Real Threats To The US Dollar's Status As The International Reserve Currency." Business Insider, Inc, 11 Nov. 2013. <http://www.businessinsider.com/dollar-as-international-reserve-currency-2013-11>.

12. Jen, Stephen. "The Opposition's Opening Remarks." *Economist Debates*. The Economist, 20 Sept. 2011. <http://www.economist.com/debate/days/view/751#con_statement_anchor>.

13. Makin, John H. "Three Dangerous Myths about Monetary Policy." American Enterprise Institute, 2 Nov. 2011. <http://www.aei.org/paper/economics/monetary-policy/federal-reserve/three-dangerous-myths-about-monetary-policy/>.

14. "Who Owns the Federal Reserve?" Federal Reserve Board. <http://www.federalreserve.gov/faqs/about_14986.htm>.

15. Grim, Ryan. "Federal Reserve Officials Leave For Wall Street With Privileged Info." The Huffington Post, 16 Apr. 2012. <http://www.huffingtonpost.com/2012/04/16/federal-reserve-officials-privileged-information-financial-crisis_n_1428957.html>.

16. Konczal, Mike. "Here's What's Wrong with Rand Paul's 'Audit the Fed' Bill." *Wonkblog*. The Washington Post, 16 Nov. 2013. <http://www.washingtonpost.com/blogs/wonkblog/wp/2013/11/16/heres-whats-wrong-with-rand-pauls-audit-the-fed-bill/>.

17. Lewis, Nathan. "Assuming We 'End The Fed,' What's The Next Step?" *Forbes*. Forbes Magazine, 28 Mar. 2013. <http://www.forbes.com/sites/nathanlewis/2013/03/28/assuming-we-end-the-fed-whats-the-next-step/>.

18. O'Harrow, Robert, Jr., and Dan Keating. "Lawmakers' Committee Assignments and Industry Investments Overlap." The Washington Post, 06 Feb. 2012. <http://www.washingtonpost.com/politics/lawmakers-committee-

assignments-and-industry-investments-
overlap/2012/01/28/gIQAUn8YYQ_story.html>.

19. Zumbrun, Joshua. "Bernanke Says Fed in 'Finest Hours' Stood Up to
    Pressure." Bloomberg, 16 Dec. 2013.
    <http://www.bloomberg.com/news/2013-12-16/bernanke-says-fed-
    in-finest-hours-resisted-political-pressure.html>.

20. Marshall, Robert. "Virginia Proposes Alternative Currency In Case Of
    Federal Reserve Collapse." Interview by Robert Siegel. National
    Public Radio, 6 Feb. 2013.
    <http://www.npr.org/2013/02/06/171310937/virginia-proposes-
    alternative-currency-in-case-of-federal-reserve-collapse>.

21. "The History of Gold and Silver." JM Bullion.
    <http://www.jmbullion.com/guide/history/>.

22. Wolman, David. "A Short History of American Money, From Fur to
    Fiat." *The Atlantic*. Atlantic Media Company, 06 Feb. 2012.
    <http://www.theatlantic.com/business/archive/2012/02/a-short-
    history-of-american-money-from-fur-to-fiat/252620/>.

23. Wolman, David. "A Short History of American Money, From Fur to
    Fiat." *The Atlantic*. Atlantic Media Company, 06 Feb. 2012.
    <http://www.theatlantic.com/business/archive/2012/02/a-short-
    history-of-american-money-from-fur-to-fiat/252620/>.

24. Goldstein, Jacob, and David Kestenbaum. "Why We Left The Gold
    Standard." National Public Radio, 21 Apr. 2011.
    <http://www.npr.org/blogs/money/2011/04/27/135604828/why-
    we-left-the-gold-standard>.

25. Rastogi, Nina S. "Production of Gold Has Many Negative
    Environmental Effects." The Washington Post, 21 Sept. 2010.
    <http://www.washingtonpost.com/wp-
    dyn/content/article/2010/09/20/AR2010092004730.html>.

26. Bhide, Amar. "Re-Decentralizing the Fed." Project Syndicate, 9 Oct.
    2013. <http://www.project-syndicate.org/commentary/amar-bhid-
    why-us-monetary-policy-should-be-decentralized>.

27. Indiviglio, Daniel. "Why We Need the Fed." *The Atlantic*. Atlantic
    Media Company, 14 Jan. 2011.
    <http://www.theatlantic.com/business/archive/2011/01/why-we-
    need-the-fed/69554/>.

28. Tseng, Nin-Hai. "Why the Fed Should Worry about Deflation."
    CNNMoney. Cable News Network, 30 Oct. 2013.
    <http://finance.fortune.cnn.com/2013/10/30/federal-reserve-
    deflation/>.

29. Chen, Tim. "American Household Credit Card Debt Statistics: 2014."
    NerdWallet, Inc., Mar. 2014.

<http://www.nerdwallet.com/blog/credit-card-data/average-credit-card-debt-household/>.

30. Constantin, Lucian. "Cybercriminals Increasingly Use Online Banking Fraud Automation Techniques." Computerworld, 26 Jan. 2012. <http://www.computerworld.com/s/article/9228527/Cybercriminals_increasingly_use_online_banking_fraud_automation_techniques>.

31. Gregg, Judd. "Financial Industry Is Serious About Cybersecurity." *BloombergView.com*. Bloomberg, 4 July 2013. <http://www.bloombergview.com/articles/2013-07-04/financial-industry-is-serious-about-cybersecurity>.

32. Yellin, Tal, Dominic Aratari, and Jose Pagliery. "What Is Bitcoin?" *CNNMoney*. Cable News Network. <http://money.cnn.com/infographic/technology/what-is-bitcoin/>.

33. "Some Things You Need to Know." *Bitcoin.org*. The Bitcoin Foundation. <https://bitcoin.org/en/you-need-to-know>.

34. Wolff, Josephine. "How Can We Stop Bitcoin Thefts and Scams?" Slate Magazine, 4 Feb. 2014. <http://www.slate.com/articles/technology/future_tense/2014/02/bitcoin_ransomware_scams_how_cryptocurrencies_threaten_our_financial_security.html>.

35. Fuller, Cameron. "Bitcoin Vs. Bank Of Finland: Cryptocurrencies Ruled As Commodities After Failing Money Test." International Business Times, 21 Jan. 2014. <http://www.ibtimes.com/bitcoin-vs-bank-finland-cryptocurrencies-ruled-commodities-after-failing-money-test-1545072>.

36. Green, Robert A. "The Tricky Business Of Taxing Bitcoin." *Forbes*. Forbes Magazine, 03 Dec. 2013. <http://www.forbes.com/sites/greatspeculations/2013/12/03/the-tricky-business-of-taxing-bitcoin/>.

37. Stein, Robert. "Citizen's Guide to Dollarization." Senate Banking Committee, July 1999. <http://www.banking.senate.gov/docs/reports/dollar.htm>.

38. Annunziata, Marco. "What Is The Current State Of The Eurozone Debt Crisis?" *Forbes*. Forbes Magazine, 16 Aug. 2013. <http://www.forbes.com/sites/quora/2013/08/16/what-is-the-current-state-of-the-eurozone-debt-crisis/>.

39. Steiner, Sheyna. "European Debt Crisis: Impact on the US." Bankrate, 29 Oct. 2012. <http://www.bankrate.com/finance/economics/european-debt-crisis-impact-on-us-1.aspx>.

40. Blinder, Alan S., and Jeremy B. Rudd. "The Supply-Shock Explanation of the Great Stagflation Revisited." National Bureau of

Economic Research. Working Paper #14563 Dec. 2008.
<http://www.nber.org/papers/w14563>.

41. "Trade Profiles: United States." World Trade Organization, Sept.
2013.
<http://stat.wto.org/CountryProfile/WSDBCountryPFView.aspx?La
nguage=S&Country=US>.

Chapter 9

1. "The Dangers of Debt: Lending Weight." The Economist, 14 Sept.
2013. <http://www.economist.com/news/schools-brief/21586284-
second-our-series-articles-financial-crisis-looks-role-debt-and>.

2. Small, Bridget. "Avoiding Debt-Relief Scams." Federal Trade
Commission, 17 Dec. 2013.
<http://www.consumer.ftc.gov/blog/avoiding-debt-relief-scams>.

3. "Slavery by Another Name." Public Broadcast Service, 13 Feb. 2012.
<http://www.pbs.org/tpt/slavery-by-another-
name/themes/peonage/>.

4. Sergie, Mohammed A., and Christopher Alessi. "The Credit Rating
Controversy." Council on Foreign Relations, 22 Oct. 2013.
<http://www.cfr.org/financial-crises/credit-rating-
controversy/p22328#p2>.

5. "Poor Standards?" The Economist, 20 Dec. 2013.
<http://www.economist.com/blogs/charlemagne/2013/12/eu-and-
credit-rating-agencies>.

6. Dorning, Mike, John Detrixhe, and Ian Katz. "The S&P Downgrade,
One Year Later." *BusinessWeek*. Bloomberg, 19 July 2012.
<http://www.businessweek.com/articles/2012-07-19/the-s-and-p-
downgrade-one-year-later>.

7. "Household Debt Service and Financial Obligations Ratios." Federal
Reserve Board, 18 Mar. 2014.
<http://www.federalreserve.gov/releases/housedebt/>.

8. Singletary, Michelle. "Mortgage Forgiveness Tax Break Needs to Be
Restored — Immediately." The Washington Post, 09 Jan. 2014.
<http://www.washingtonpost.com/business/mortgage-forgiveness-
tax-break-needs-to-be-restored--immediately/2014/01/07/5c2d2bfa-
77df-11e3-8963-b4b654bcc9b2_story.html>.

9. "Recession's Surprise Impact on Credit Scores." *MarketWatch*. The
Wall Street Journal, 17 July 2012.
<http://www.marketwatch.com/story/recessions-surprise-impact-on-
credit-scores-1342532155897>.

10. Singletary, Michelle. "Mortgage Forgiveness Tax Break Needs to Be Restored — Immediately." The Washington Post, 09 Jan. 2014. <http://www.washingtonpost.com/business/mortgage-forgiveness-tax-break-needs-to-be-restored--immediately/2014/01/07/5c2d2bfa-77df-11e3-8963-b4b654bcc9b2_story.html>.

11. Dynan, Karen. "Is a Household Debt Overhang Holding Back Consumption?" The Brookings Institution, Spring 2012. <http://www.brookings.edu/research/papers/2012/09/debt-overhang-dynan>.

12. "Earnings and Unemployment Rates by Educational Attainment." U.S. Bureau of Labor Statistics, 24 Mar. 2014. <http://www.bls.gov/emp/ep_chart_001.htm>.

13. Denhart, Chris. "How The $1.2 Trillion College Debt Crisis Is Crippling Students, Parents And The Economy." *Forbes*. Forbes Magazine, 07 Aug. 2013. <http://www.forbes.com/sites/specialfeatures/2013/08/07/how-the-college-debt-is-crippling-students-parents-and-the-economy/>.

14. Leonhardt, David. "Why Does College Cost So Much?" *Economix*. The New York Times, 18 Feb. 2011. <http://economix.blogs.nytimes.com/2011/02/18/why-does-college-cost-so-much/>.

15. Hilsinger, Claire. "Up, Up And Away: College Tuition Is On The Rise." *Forbes*. Forbes Magazine, 24 July 2013. <http://www.forbes.com/sites/specialfeatures/2013/07/24/up-up-and-away-college-tuition-is-on-the-rise/>.

16. "SHEF - State Higher Education Finance FY12." State Higher Education Executive Officers Association, 6 Mar. 2013. <http://www.sheeo.org/node/631>.

17. Marklein, Mary B. "Colleges See a Slowdown in Tuition Price Increases." *USA Today*. Gannett, 23 Oct. 2013. <http://www.usatoday.com/story/news/nation/2013/10/23/college-tuitions-rising-more-slowly/3151897/>.

18. "Ensuring That Student Loans Are Affordable." The White House. <http://www.whitehouse.gov/issues/education/higher-education/ensuring-that-student-loans-are-affordable>.

19. "The Debt to the Penny and Who Holds It." *Treasury Direct*. Department of the Treasury, 28 Mar. 2014. <http://www.treasurydirect.gov/NP/debt/current>.

20. "Historical Debt Outstanding - Annual 2000 - 2012." *Treasury Direct*. Department of the Treasury. <http://www.treasurydirect.gov/govt/reports/pd/histdebt/histdebt_histo5.htm>.

21. David N. Weil, "Fiscal Policy." *The Concise Encyclopedia of Economics.* 2008. Library of Economics and Liberty. <http://www.econlib.org/library/Enc/FiscalPolicy.html>.

22. Cohen, Jon, and Sean Sullivan. "Cut Government Spending? Sure....in Theory." *The Fix.* The Washington Post, 6 Mar. 2013. <http://www.washingtonpost.com/blogs/the-fix/wp/2013/03/06/cut-government-spending-sure-cut-the-military-no-way/>.

23. "Policy Basics: Where Do Our Federal Tax Dollars Go? —." Center on Budget and Policy Priorities, 12 Apr. 2013. <http://www.cbpp.org/cms/?fa=view&id=1258>.

24. Jaffe, Greg. "Defense Secretary Hagel Defends the Pentagon's Proposed Budget and Cuts." The Washington Post, 05 Mar. 2014. <http://www.washingtonpost.com/world/national-security/defense-secretary-hagel-defends-the-pentagons-proposed-budget-and-cuts/2014/03/05/c5c9a002-a480-11e3-84d4-e59b1709222c_story.html>.

25. Ohlemacher, Stephen. "Social Security Fund Will Be Drained by 2037." *MSNBC.* NBCUniversal, 27 Jan. 2011. <http://www.nbcnews.com/id/41293592/ns/politics-more_politics/t/social-security-fund-will-be-drained/#.Uzh4yV4zh7w>.

26. Teal, Gary. "How Accurate Is The Concern That Social Security Money Will One Day Run Out?" *Forbes.* Forbes Magazine, 28 Aug. 2013. <http://www.forbes.com/sites/quora/2013/08/28/how-accurate-is-the-concern-that-social-security-money-will-one-day-run-out/>.

27. Goldfarb, Zachary A. "Study: U.S. Poverty Rate Decreased over past Half-century Thanks to Safety-net Programs." The Washington Post, 10 Dec. 2013. <http://www.washingtonpost.com/business/economy/study-us-poverty-rate-decreased-over-past-half-century-thanks-to-safety-net-programs/2013/12/09/9322c834-60f3-11e3-94ad-004fefa61ee6_story.html>.

28. "Discretionary Spending." The Concord Coalition, Jan. 2012. <http://www.concordcoalition.org/issues/indicators/discretionary-spending>.

29. French, Lauren. "Obama Re-ups Corporate Tax Reform Call." POLITICO, 28 Jan. 2014. <http://www.politico.com/blogs/politico-live/2014/01/obama-reups-corporate-tax-reform-call-182148.html>.

Chapter 10

1. "Crisis Squeezes Income and Puts Pressure on Inequality and Poverty in the OECD." Organisation for Economic Co-operation and Development, 11 July 2013.
<http://www.oecd.org/social/inequality.htm>.

2. Goldfarb, Zachary A. "Obama Focuses Agenda on Relieving Economic Inequality." The Washington Post, 05 Dec. 2013.
<http://www.washingtonpost.com/politics/obama-focuses-agenda-on-relieving-economic-inequality/2013/12/04/bef286ac-5cfc-11e3-be07-006c776266ed_story.html>.

3. Ungar, Rick. "The Truth About The Bush Tax Cuts And Job Growth." *Forbes*. Forbes Magazine, 17 July 2012.
<http://www.forbes.com/sites/rickungar/2012/07/17/the-truth-about-the-bush-tax-cuts-and-job-growth/>.

4. Smith, Elliot B., and Phil Kuntz. "Disclosed: The Pay Gap Between CEOs and Employees." *BusinessWeek*. Bloomberg, 02 May 2013.
<http://www.businessweek.com/articles/2013-05-02/disclosed-the-pay-gap-between-ceos-and-employees>.

5. "Why C.E.O. Pay Keeps Going Up." *Open Season*. The New Yorker, 21 Oct. 2013.
<http://www.newyorker.com/talk/financial/2013/10/21/131021ta_talk_surowiecki>.

6. Rollert, John P. "Sleight of the 'Invisible Hand'." The New York Times, 21 Oct. 2012.
<http://opinionator.blogs.nytimes.com/2012/10/21/sleight-of-the-invisible-hand/>.

7. Tankersley, Jim. "Yes, the Middle Class Really Is Falling behind." *Wonkblog*. The Washington Post, 24 Jan. 2013.
<http://www.washingtonpost.com/blogs/wonkblog/wp/2013/01/24/yes-the-middle-class-really-is-falling-behind/>.

8. Ostry, Jonathan D., Andrew Berg, and Charalambos G. Tsangarides. *Redistribution, Inequality, and Growth*. International Monetary Fund, 2014.
<http://www.imf.org/external/pubs/ft/sdn/2014/sdn1402.pdf>

9. Isaacs, Julia B. "International Comparisons of Economic Mobility." The Brookings Institution, Feb. 2008.
<http://www.brookings.edu/research/reports/2008/02/economic-mobility-sawhill>.

10. Strauss, Valerie. "Five Stereotypes about Poor Families and Education." The Washington Post, 28 Oct. 2013.
<http://www.washingtonpost.com/blogs/answer-

sheet/wp/2013/10/28/five-stereotypes-about-poor-families-and-education/>.

11. Seitles, Marc. "Perpetuation of Residential Racial Segregation in America: Historical Discrimination, Modern Forms of Exclusion, and Inclusionary Remedies, The." *J. Land Use & Envtl. L.* 14 (1998): 89. <http://dev.law.fsu.edu/journals/landuse/Vol141/seit.htm>

12. Edelman, Peter. "Poverty in America: Why Can't We End It?" The New York Times, 28 July 2012. <http://www.nytimes.com/2012/07/29/opinion/sunday/why-cant-we-end-poverty-in-america.html>.

13. Greek, Cecil E. "Crime, Poverty, and Economic Inequality." Florida State University. <http://www.criminology.fsu.edu/crimtheory/poverty.htm>.

14. Raab, Barbara. "Key to Climbing out of Poverty: Location, Location, Location." NBC News, 23 July 2013. <http://www.nbcnews.com/news/other/key-climbing-out-poverty-location-location-location-f6C10713806>.

15. "Are We Helping the Poor?" The Economist, 18 Dec. 2013. <http://www.economist.com/blogs/democracyinamerica/2013/12/anti-poverty-programmes>.

16. Greenstone, Michael, Adam Looney, Jeremy Patashnik, and Muxin Yu. "Thirteen Economic Facts about Social Mobility and the Role of Education." *The Hamilton Project.* The Brookings Institution, June 2013. <http://www.brookings.edu/research/reports/2013/06/13-facts-higher-education>.

17. "Higher Education: Gaps in Access and Persistence Study." *National Center for Education Statistics.* Institute of Education Studies, Aug. 2012. <http://nces.ed.gov/pubs2012/2012046/index.asp>.

18. Plumer, Brad. "How the Recession Turned Middle-class Jobs into Low-wage Jobs." *Wonkblog.* The Washington Post, 28 Feb. 2013. <http://www.washingtonpost.com/blogs/wonkblog/wp/2013/02/28/how-the-recession-turned-middle-class-jobs-into-low-wage-jobs/>.

19. Reardon, Sean F. "The widening academic achievement gap between the rich and the poor: New evidence and possible explanations." *Whither opportunity* (2011): 91-116. <http://cepa.stanford.edu/content/widening-academic-achievement-gap-between-rich-and-poor-new-evidence-and-possible>

20. Brancaccio, David. "Technology Increases Divide between Rich and Poor Students: Report." *Marketplace.org.* American Public Media, 28 Feb. 2013. <http://www.marketplace.org/topics/tech/education/technology-increases-divide-between-rich-and-poor-students-report>.

21. Chetty, Raj, Nathaniel Hendren, Patrick Kline, Emmanuel Saez, and Nicholas Turner. "Is the United States Still a Land of Opportunity? Recent Trends in Intergenerational Mobility." National Bureau of Economic Research. Working Paper #19844, 22 Jan. 2014. <http://www.nber.org/papers/w19844>.

22. Chetty, Raj, Nathaniel Hendren, Patrick Kline, and Emmanuel Saez. " Where is the Land of Opportunity? The Geography of Intergenerational Mobility in the United States" National Bureau of Economic Research. Working Paper #19843, 22 Jan. 2014. <http://www.nber.org/papers/w19843>.

23. Deaton, Angus. "Policy implications of the gradient of health and wealth." *Health Affairs* 21.2 (2002): 13-30. <http://www.ncbi.nlm.nih.gov/pubmed/11900153>

24. Austin, Michael J., and Kathy Lemon. "Promising programs to serve low-income families in poverty neighborhoods." *Journal of health & social policy* 21.1 (2006): 65-94. < http://www.ncbi.nlm.nih.gov/pubmed/16418128>

25. Boushey, Heather. "Middle Class Series: Economic Inequality Is Not Sustainable." Center for American Progress, 6 Dec. 2011. <http://www.americanprogress.org/issues/economy/news/2011/12/06/10792/economic-inequality-is-not-sustainable/>.

26. Berman, Jillian. "Raising Taxes On The Rich Would Reduce Income Inequality: Larry Summers." The Huffington Post, 17 Feb. 2014. <http://www.huffingtonpost.com/2014/02/17/taxes-rich-larry-summers_n_4804285.html>.

27. Foster, J.D., and Curtis Dubay. "Of Course Higher Taxes Slow Growth." *The Foundry*. The Heritage Foundation, 25 Apr. 2012. <http://blog.heritage.org/2012/04/25/of-course-higher-taxes-slow-growth-a-response-to-diamond-and-saez/>.

28. Kaufman, Alexander. "IMF Issues Income Inequality Warning, Suggests Ways To Slow It." The Huffington Post, 13 Mar. 2014. <http://www.huffingtonpost.com/2014/03/13/imf-inequality-income_n_4958498.html>.

29. Boushey, Heather. "Understanding How Raising the Federal Minimum Wage Affects Income Inequality and Economic Growth." Washington Center for Equitable Growth, 12 Mar. 2014. <http://equitablegrowth.org/work/understanding-the-minimum-wage-and-income-inequality-and-economic-growth>.

30. "The Argument in the Floor." The Economist, 24 Nov. 2012. <http://www.economist.com/news/finance-and-economics/21567072-evidence-mounting-moderate-minimum-wages-can-do-more-good-harm>.

31. Konczal, Mike. "Thinking Utopian: How about a Universal Basic Income?" *Wonkblog*. The Washington Post, 11 May 2013. <http://www.washingtonpost.com/blogs/wonkblog/wp/2013/05/11/thinking-utopian-how-about-a-universal-basic-income/>.

32. "Promoting Pro-Poor Growth: Private Sector Development." Organisation for Economic Co-operation and Development, 2006. <http://www.oecd.org/dac/povertyreduction/promotingpro-poorgrowthprivatesectordevelopment.htm>.

33. Carnegie, Andrew. "Wealth." *North American Review*, June 1889. <http://www.swarthmore.edu/SocSci/rbannis1/AIH19th/Carnegie.html>.

Chapter 11

1. "Economic Benefits of Wetlands." Environmental Protection Agency, Mar. 2006. <http://water.epa.gov/type/wetlands/upload/wetlands-economic-benefits.pdf>.

2. "New Study Shows Climate Change Largely Irreversible." National Oceanic and Atmospheric Administration, 26 Jan. 2009. <http://www.noaanews.noaa.gov/stories2009/20090126_climate.html>.

3. Anderegg, William RL, et al. "Expert credibility in climate change." *Proceedings of the National Academy of Sciences* 107.27 (2010): 12107-12109. <http://www.pnas.org/content/107/27/12107.short>

4. "Climate Change in the American Mind: Americans' Global Warming Beliefs and Attitudes in November 2013." *Yale Project on Climate Change Communication*. Yale University, Nov. 2013. <http://environment.yale.edu/climate-communication/article/Climate-Beliefs-November-2013>.ABS Dunlap Study

5. Masters, Jeff. "The Manufactured Doubt Industry and the Hacked Email Controversy." Weather Underground, 25 Nov. 2009. <http://www.wunderground.com/blog/JeffMasters/comment.html?entrynum=1389>.

6. Germain, Tiffany, Ryan Koronowski, and Jeff Spross. "The Anti-Science Climate Denier Caucus: 113th Congress Edition." *ThinkProgress*. Center for American Progress, 26 June 2013. <http://thinkprogress.org/climate/2013/06/26/2202141/anti-science-climate-denier-caucus-113th-congress-edition/>.

7. "Teens View Climate Change as Solvable, But See Problems Handed Off to Them by Current Leaders." *Planet Change*. The Nature Conservancy, 9 Sept. 2011.

<http://change.nature.org/2011/09/09/teens-view-climate-change-as-solvable-but-see-problems-handed-off-to-them-by-current-leaders/>.

8. McLamb, Eric. "The Ecological Impact of the Industrial Revolution." Ecology Global Network, 18 Sept. 2011. <http://www.ecology.com/2011/09/18/ecological-impact-industrial-revolution/>.

9. Rodrigue, Jean-Paul. "Externalities of Air Pollution." Hofstra University, 2013. <http://people.hofstra.edu/geotrans/eng/ch8en/conc8en/table_airpollutionexternalities.html>.

10. "The Hidden Cost of Fossil Fuels." Union of Concerned Scientists, 29 Oct. 2002. <http://www.ucsusa.org/clean_energy/our-energy-choices/coal-and-other-fossil-fuels/the-hidden-cost-of-fossil.html>.

11. Goad, Jessica, and Christy Goldfuss. "Drilling Could Threaten Our National Parks." Center for American Progress, 12 Sept. 2012. <http://www.americanprogress.org/issues/green/news/2012/09/12/37152/drilling-could-threaten-our-national-parks/>.

12. Colman, Zack. "Report Finds US Energy Production Growing, Consumption down." The Hill, 26 Dec. 2012. <http://thehill.com/blogs/e2-wire/e2-wire/274569-eia-us-energy-consumption-down-production-up>.

13. Tuttle, Brad R. "Why the Era of High Gas Prices Is Supposedly Ending." Time, 19 Dec. 2013. <http://business.time.com/2013/12/19/why-the-era-of-high-gas-prices-is-supposedly-ending/>.

14. Plumer, Brad. "Here's Why Central Appalachia's Coal Industry Is Dying." *Wonkblog*. The Washington Post, 4 Nov. 2013. <http://www.washingtonpost.com/blogs/wonkblog/wp/2013/11/04/heres-why-central-appalachias-coal-industry-is-dying/>.

15. Koch, Wendy. "U.S. Forecasts Natural Gas Boom through 2040." *USA Today*. Gannett, 16 Dec. 2013. <http://www.usatoday.com/story/news/nation/2013/12/16/doe-forecast-natural-gas-boom/4034723/>.

16. Ward, Matthew L. "Hurdles for a Natural Gas Transition." The New York Times, 8 July 2010. <http://green.blogs.nytimes.com/2010/07/08/hurdles-for-a-natural-gas-transition/>.

17. Schrope, Mark. "Fracking Outpaces Science on Its Impact." *Environment Yale*. Yale University, 2012. <http://environment.yale.edu/envy/stories/fracking-outpaces-science-on-its-impact>.

18. "Climate Change 2014: Impacts, Adaptation, and Vulnerability." Intergovernmental Panel on Climate Change, 30 Mar. 2014. <http://ipcc-wg2.gov/AR5/images/uploads/IPCC_WG2AR5_SPM_Approved.pdf>.

19. "Total Carbon Dioxide Emissions from the Consumption of Energy." *International Energy Statistics*. Department of Energy, 2012. <http://www.eia.gov/cfapps/ipdbproject/IEDIndex3.cfm?tid=90&pid=44&aid=8>.

20. "Transportation Sector Energy Consumption." *U.S. Energy Information Administration (EIA)*. Department of Energy, 25 July 2012. <http://www.eia.gov/forecasts/ieo/transportation.cfm>.

21. "Annual Energy Review - Total Energy." *U.S. Energy Information Administration (EIA)*. Department of Energy, 27 Sept. 2012. <http://www.eia.gov/totalenergy/data/annual/pecss_diagram.cfm>.

22. "Why American Transport Projects Cost so Much." The Economist, 09 Sept. 2012. <http://www.economist.com/blogs/gulliver/2012/09/public-transport-costs>.

23. Richard L. Stroup, "Free-Market Environmentalism." *The Concise Encyclopedia of Economics*. 2008. Library of Economics and Liberty. <http://www.econlib.org/library/Enc/FreeMarketEnvironmentalism.html>.

24. Graff Zivin, Joshua, and Matthew Neidell. "The impact of pollution on worker productivity." *American Economic Review* 102 (2012): 3652-3673. <http://www.nber.org/papers/w17004>

25. Bullard, Robert D. "Poverty, Pollution and Environmental Racism: Strategies for Building Healthy and Sustainable Communities." *Environmental Justice Resource Center*. Clark Atlanta University, 2 July 2002. <http://www.ejrc.cau.edu/PovpolEj.html>.

26. Syed, Tajdarul H., et al. "Satellite-based global-ocean mass balance estimates of interannual variability and emerging trends in continental freshwater discharge." *Proceedings of the National Academy of Sciences* 107.42 (2010): 17916-17921. <http://www.pnas.org/content/early/2010/09/28/1003292107>

27. "Climate Change Impacts and Adapting to Change." Environmental Protection Agency, 18 Mar. 2014. <http://www.epa.gov/climatechange/impacts-adaptation/>.

28. "You're Going to Get Wet." The Economist, 15 June 2013. <http://www.economist.com/news/united-states/21579470-americans-are-building-beachfront-homes-even-oceans-rise-youre-going-get-wet>.

29. "Agriculture and Food Supply Impacts & Adaptation." Environmental Protection Agency, 9 Sept. 2013. <http://www.epa.gov/climatechange/impacts-adaptation/agriculture.html>.

30. "The Potential Impacts of Climate Change on U.S. Transportation." Transportation Research Board, May-June 2008. <http://www.trb.org/Main/Blurbs/The_Potential_Impacts_of_Climate_Change_on_US_Tran_156825.aspx>.

31. "Limiting the Federal Government's Fiscal Exposure by Better Managing Climate Change Risks." Government Accountability Office, 14 Feb. 2013. <http://www.gao.gov/highrisk/limiting_federal_government_fiscal_exposure/why_did_study#t=1>.

32. Gale, William G. "The Tax Favored By Most Economists." The Brookings Institution, 12 Mar. 2013. <http://www.brookings.edu/research/opinions/2013/03/12-taxing-carbon-gale>.

33. Mufson, Steven. "On Campuses, a Fossil-fuel Divestment Movement." The Washington Post, 25 Nov. 2013. <http://www.washingtonpost.com/business/economy/on-campuses-a-fossil-fuel-divestment-movement/2013/11/25/45a545e6-52fc-11e3-a7f0-b790929232e1_story.html>.

About the Author

Evan M. Baumel

Evan Baumel (born 1992) is a public policy writer who has experience in non-profit advocacy and Congressional affairs. He received his Bachelor of Arts in Communications, Legal Studies, Economics, and Government (CLEG) from American University's School of Public Affairs.

Baumel has a strong background in political communications and public policy. He has contributed to a variety of blogs and periodicals on issues including the environment, health care, economics, law, and social media.

Coming to DC from Florida, Baumel has come to appreciate the political atmosphere of Washington, DC. His experience on Capitol Hill has provided him a unique perspective of policies crafted by our members of Congress and their staff. This knowledge has culminated into his first literary venture, *Broken Mast: Changing Course for the Capitalist Ship*, which covers the greatest challenges to economic growth in the current marketplace.

Evan currently lives in Washington, DC. You can find out more information about the author and his work at www.evanbaumel.com.

www.ingramcontent.com/pod-product-compliance
Lightning Source LLC
Chambersburg PA
CBHW022108280326
4193.3CB00007B/299